BARRIOR

BARRIOR

TIMOTHY MIRANDA, ESQ.

IF SOMEONE LIKE ME CAN PASS THE TOUGHEST BAR EXAMINATION IN THE COUNTRY ON THE FIRST ATTEMPT, SOMEONE LIKE YOU HAS NO EXCUSE TO FAIL!

ANECDOTES, STRATEGY AND CANDID INSIGHT FOR A BABY BAR OR BAR EXAMINATION <u>BEATDOWN</u>.

Miranda Law Group, PC

The opinions expressed in this manuscript are solely the opinions of the author and do not represent the opinions or thoughts of the publisher. The author has represented and warranted full ownership and/or legal right to publish all the materials in this book.

Barrior
If someone like me can pass the toughest bar examination in the country on the first attempt, someone like you has no excuse to fail! Anecdotes, strategy and candid insight for a baby bar or bar examination beatdown.
All Rights Reserved.
Copyright © 2011 Timothy Miranda, Esq.
v3.0, r1.0

Cover Photo © 2011 JupiterImages Corporation. All rights reserved - used with permission.

This book may not be reproduced, transmitted, or stored in whole or in part by any means, including graphic, electronic, or mechanical without the express written consent of the publisher except in the case of brief quotations embodied in critical articles and reviews.

ISBN: 978-0-578-09011-5

PRINTED IN THE UNITED STATES OF AMERICA

Dedication

This book is dedicated to everyone who ever laughed (behind my back) when they first found out that I was attending a correspondence law school.

This book is dedicated to everyone who never laughed when they first found out that I was attending a correspondence law school.

Special Thanks

GES, Esq.
HJB, Esq.
RDD, Esq.

100% SATISFACTION GUARANTEED—
PASS OR DON'T PAY!

Subject to the terms and conditions delineated below, should you purchase this book and not pass your subsequent Baby Bar or Bar Examination for whatever reason, **simply return the book to me to receive a 100 percent refund of the purchase price!**

<u>Terms and Conditions</u>
The foregoing offer is illusory at best and, therefore, is incapable of creating a power of acceptance in the offeree. Notwithstanding, the offeror is the master of his offer and therefore said illusory offer is hereby revoked. If you are already even considering the prospects of failing the Baby Bar or Bar Examination, then you are already failing the Baby Bar or Bar Examination. Check yourself before you wreck yourself.

Table of Content

Pre-Fuss 1
A few words before a lot of words

Blundergrad 3
Pre-law? Really?

Law Skewer 11
Law school? Really?

I of the Tiger 15
Bar Card blinders

Certified Law Jerk 19
All work, no pay

I'll Take 2 29
February or July?

Beginner Schmuck 33
Go luck yourself

Bar Revue 37
It's only money

The Art of Bar 41
All war is based on deception

Stratustician 47
Gray skies turn blue

Audio Files 53
Rush hour of power

Exercism 57
Sweat with small stuff

The May Tricks 59
If you predict essays, I predict victory

Checkered Passed 69
Don't be a looky-loser

¿Que Passit Essay? 77
There is no mañana

PT Loser 87
It's no joyride

Multistaid 97
150 raw score on a bad day

The Harangueover 107
A few more words after a lot of words

The Cradle Will Fall 111
Baby Bar regimen

See, Be, Esq. 113
CBX regimen

Pre-Fuss

BARRIOR IS NOT a misspelling of barrier (I'm a lawyer), nor is it a homage to my old neighborhood. Rather, a Barrior is a Bar warrior, a Bar candidate or law student that has the guts, dedication, and hustle to take the fight to the Baby Bar or Bar Examination, beating the ominous statistics, rather than being beaten by them. A Barrior is someone like me, and, hopefully, someone like you.

This book is a candid introspection of my unlikely trajectory from layman to lawyer in California, the state that is ubiquitously regarded as having the toughest Bar Examination in the country. What makes it a worthwhile read is that I never received a traditional undergraduate degree, and likewise, did my law school entirely from home, all while juggling a career, a failed career, and then a new start-up venture. To put it another way, if I can turn a Juris Doctor from a barber college-esque law school into a successful first-time pass on the Baby Bar and then on the California Bar Examination, *you better pass*.

As the gist of this book is inspiration vis-à-vis anecdotal and strategic prose, my proselytizing is transferrable to any Bar Examination in any jurisdiction. Even so, and while it may be counterproductive for me to say this, you should not waste your precious pre-Bar Examination time reading this book unless you are going to make the most out of it by following my lead and working your ass off. No matter what anyone else may say in order to hawk their wares, there simply is no way to pass the Baby Bar or Bar Examination, either as a first-time taker or repeater, without an all-in Barrior mentality.

Timothy Miranda, Esq.
Barrior and Barrister

Blundergrad

I WAS A spry 35 years old when a friend of mine first told me that you could become a lawyer in California by successfully completing an unaccredited correspondence law school program, even without an undergraduate degree. Better still was the fact that no Law School Admission Test ("LSAT") exam was required and the whole course was equivalent in cost to one semester at a traditional law school. Since I lived in California and had dropped out of college in my junior year, the prospect of becoming a lawyer from my living room truly piqued my interest.

You see, back when I was in high school, I had often considered becoming a lawyer, predominantly based upon what I had seen on television and the movies. Given my innate knack for debate and oratory (arguing) as well as an overarching interest in making money and wearing a white collar, being a lawyer seemed like it would be an ideal fit for me. Even more compelling to me at the time was the fact that these lawyers I had seen on television and the movies always seemed to drive nice cars, dress well, and undress nice women.

Since I was obviously a shallow young man with a warped sense of reality, it should come as no surprise that in spite of my good grades and having been accepted for admission to a couple of decent universities, I opted to enroll in the local community college upon graduation from high school. While the curriculum in community college is generally solid, and community college provides an accessible, cost-effective means of obtaining an education, my primary motivation in eschewing a 4-year university was to stay close to home and keep hanging out with my friends, most of whom had also enrolled in the same community college. Theoretically, I had planned on transferring to one of the foregoing universities in my junior year, with the goal of ultimately receiving a bachelor's degree in business administration.

As I started to study subjects in junior college such as economics, entrepreneurialism became increasingly interesting to me. Aside from the obvious profit motive, I found it captivating that one could transform an idea into an enterprise, creating something out of nothing. Equally entrancing was the fact that one who starts their own company can sidestep the corporate ladder and ascend directly to the top rung. For this reason, when I was 19 years old, I did what you would expect any student living in sunny Southern California to do—I started a ski pole business.

Forgetting for a moment the fact that I was only an intermediate skier who had no real snow or mountains of any significance in close proximity, and further forgetting the fact that this was a time when snowboarding was just starting to really take off, meaning that interest in skiing was really starting to wane, I decided to follow my heart and just go for it in spite of what the traditional market factors may have indicated. To me, one of the primary reasons why snowboarding was gaining in popularity so quickly was its irreverence, whereas skiing seemed stuck in its stodgy ways of the past. "Going for it" to me meant thinking outside of the box, introducing an equally irreverent product to the skiing side of the mountain.

One of my good friends at the time, himself a less-than-an-intermediate skier, yet hailing from a wealthy family, seemed to be a perfect person to pitch my idea to. Aside from the possibility of capital contribution, he was also majoring in business administration at one of the more prestigious universities in town and had an equal interest in the profit motive.

My idea was to make a new (revolutionary) type of ski pole that was unconventional in both form and function. Since winter sports equipment is beyond the scope of this book, suffice it to say that the poles were comprised of a series of aesthetically placed bends, a safer yet more effective tip for penetrating the ice and snow as well as an integrated grip-to-glove component. Some were aluminum, and some were made of lighter composite materials. All of them ultimately sucked.

Starting a business, especially a bad business, requires a lot of capital. I was initially able to secure some financing from my family, but when that well ran dry, I had to start working, then working some more. It's really hard to make it to all of your classes when you are working so much ...

A girl that I was dating at the time happened to work for a telemarketing boiler room. She was not a telemarketer, but rather a secretary or some other nonsales-capacity employee, like eye candy for the owner. Either way, this was a good thing since the place was a fraud that ultimately got taken down by the feds. What's relevant here is that she would tell me about the kinds of cash they were throwing around, the motor pool of exotics in the company parking lot, and all the other ostentatious accoutrements of scofflaws gone wild.

Since the money was drying up fast on my end, I tried my hand at telemarketing but just couldn't do it, at least not the way they were doing it in this place. Essentially, these nice fellows were running a "1-in-4" promotion (scam) on geriatrics, promising that for a payment of thousands of dollars to cover the "taxes," people (victims) were guaranteed to win one of four great prizes. If the "winner" sent in a check for $10,000, for example, they might win a pendant or something else that was worth maybe $1,000. After a partial day's stint, I never went back after lunch. It was fortuitous that I couldn't do this job, literally or figuratively, since that raid I just mentioned transpired a couple of months later!

I bounced around a couple of other customer-service jobs until I saw an ad from a telecommunications company that was looking for a customer-service manager that was bilingual and had a college degree. Since I had some rudiments of Spanish and a partial degree in progress, I figured I could be "that guy." Oh yeah, by this time, now in my junior year, I had quit attending all of my classes so that I could work full-time to support my superstellar ski pole sensation of a business.

When they interviewed me at this place I think they liked the way I looked in a suit more than my résumé, which, at this point, was a piece of hyperbolic rubbish. Nobody checked out my references, and the girl in HR that was supposed to test my fluency in Spanish just said a couple of basic things, and then proceeded to ask me if I had a girlfriend. About a week after I had been hired as "that guy," the owner of the company had summoned me for a meeting. Apparently he had heard that there was this bilingual new guy who looked good in a suit that seemed to have a lot of potential. Ostensibly, he wanted to discuss my future with the company, but in reality, he wanted to size me up and tear me down.

It was about 6:00 p.m. on a Friday afternoon when his secretary called me and asked me to come to his office, which meant that I had to go to another building across the street. This place was growing so fast that the only office space that they could find was in two separate buildings, and this guy was in the nicer one of the two, with the saltwater fish tanks and musical water feature in the courtyard. When I walked in to the dimly lit, massive office of this person I had never met before, he was seated behind a desk. He was wearing shorts, sandals, a tee shirt with holes in it, and a salad which must have been really tasty, since he couldn't stop shoving it into his piehole while he was barking at a couple of other flunkies that were present.

Rather than say hello or introduce himself to me, I was directed to sit down in one of the two chairs in front of the desk (hot seat) while the other people that were present in the peanut gallery hovered behind me. While still scarfing that salad, he started asking me questions about my background and asked me to say some things in Spanish, even though he himself did not speak Spanish. He then asked me how my classes were going, given that I was working for him full-time and must not even have time for sleep.

My résumé at that time mentioned my majoring in business administration, which technically was true, since my recent failure to attend classes was intended to be a temporary, not permanent, development. Since the woman in Human Resources that hired me never sought clarification regarding my matriculation, I never saw the need to provide any.

Before I could spit out something clever in an attempt to deflect or mitigate the blow of his question, he started shouting, "Don't fucking lie to me. I told HR to hire a manager with a college degree and that can speak Spanish. It seems like you can speak Spanish, but you must not have a degree if you are only 'majoring' in business. Then again, you must not even be majoring in business if you are here working 10 fucking hours a day." Talk about a misguided attack; he should have saved the bravado for all those other, less ambitious employees (pikers) who weren't even around at 6:00 p.m. on a Friday.

"Look, motherfucker," he said in a voice one notch below shouting, "I am going to have HR call that school Monday morning, and if you aren't really close to finishing your degree, you're fucking fired. I want a manager with a college degree or pretty fucking close to it. If you tell me the truth that you aren't going to school right now, or if you never even went to school, you at least have a chance of keeping your fucking job." I can remember at this point being shocked by the barrage of vulgarity, yet contemporaneously impressed by this prick's ebullient diatribe.

This was a really embarrassing moment, yet I knew that a lie would be futile and that moreover, I needed the job more than my pride. I proceeded to tell him the truth, the truth being that I almost had a degree but hadn't yet finished school because of my pecuniary problems related to a start-up gone down in flames. After accomplishing his goal of humiliating me as well as demonstrating to his other cronies that he was omniscient, I ultimately got a promotion and began running the sales department. My guess is that on a visceral level, he appreciated the fact that I had the intestinal fortitude to start my own business at a relatively young age, and likewise, that I would apply for a job that was above my pay grade.

Ironically, the bulk of the sales were conducted via telemarketing, and while this company never got raided, it probably should have at least been investigated. I found out later that the owner was a convicted felon, a fact that was buried as a one-liner entitled "Other Matters" in the Management section of the company's Form S-1 filing with the Securities and Exchange Commission. Conspiracy to traffic narcotics was the conviction.

While things were starting to get better for me economically, particularly since I was a better telemarketing manager than telemarketer, this place was the worst company on the face of the earth. The same felon-owner ran that place with fear and intimidation, which most everyone put up with because they paid so well. After a while, I couldn't handle being called an "asshole" anymore and ultimately started my own telemarketing company, selling, among other things, telecommunications services on behalf of the aforementioned worst company. Ski poles were becoming a distant memory. Unfortunately, so too was my schooling.

Rather than open my telemarketing company in my hometown where the rents and wages were high, I went to a neighboring, rural county where the rents and wages were low. I had some modest capital for start-up, but in order to conserve cash, I would wear multiple hats around that place. From CEO to janitor I would work 15 hours per day, and at night, I would abut two of my telemarketing workstations together in order to create a flat surface off of the floor so that I could put a sleeping bag on top. Sleeping in my office, I enrolled in the local gym so that I could get up at 5:00 a.m. and go take a shower before starting all over again.

After about 6 months, things started to work themselves out and the entrepreneurial dream was becoming a reality. Then it became a nightmare.

Even though I had emerged as the most prolific sales agency marketing the services of the worst company on the face of the earth, my hard work on their behalf was ultimately all for not. One Friday, the president of the company, some smooth-talking guy that looked like a graying Ronald McDonald, called me at 5:00 p.m. to tell me to stop selling for them, as they were no longer going to be acquiring new customers. It turns out that they had some serious regulatory problems (surprise). Perhaps more of a surprise was the fact that after all of that initial bluster, the owner didn't even have the balls to call me himself. Prick.

This was bad news for my business, and ultimately proved nearly fatal, when they refused to pay me all of the monies I was owed, even though I had to pay all of my employees all of the monies I owed them. Not being a lawyer, and not having money for a lawyer, I ultimately settled with them for a pittance, just so that I could cover the rent payment on my office.

On bankruptcy's doorstep, I was ultimately able to resurrect the business with a new series of clients, and then sold it off in order to take a position with one of these very clients. The company was an upstart that was growing rapidly, and the fact that it was headquartered back in my hometown meant that I could get back to urban civilization. I also figured (erroneously) that the compensation package, including equity, would ultimately be worth my regression from master to servant. I was wrong. When they initially relegated me to a cubicle, it should have been a bad sign.

However, within 3 years I became a vice president of this company and had moved in to a big corner office. Within 5 years, I became the president of the international subsidiary of this company and had a big corner office in every building that I worked out of.

Within 10 years, when I was in my first year of law school, the company collapsed under the weight of its own debt and the founder's myopia. I remember him calling me on a Friday afternoon, telling me that on the following Monday morning the doors would close and we would all be out of a job.

I need to stop answering the phone on Friday afternoon, I thought to myself.

As a paradoxical aside, I never again spoke to my ski business partner-friend after he sent me a certified letter which effectually stated that he was making a unilateral decision to assume the "company." When I did speak with his sister several years later, she told me that he had eventually gone on to study law at the best law school in town, and yet, somehow, failed the California Bar Examination ("CBX") after *multiple* attempts, and ultimately gave up trying to become a lawyer.

Maybe he kept getting a Corporations essay regarding fiduciary duties of directors and shareholder rights.

Law Skewer

EVEN THOUGH I turned my junior college dropout into a relatively successful run as an entrepreneur and telecommunications executive, the fact that I had set my collegiate sights so low, only to ultimately look away completely and never complete college, always haunted me. I literally used to have a recurring nightmare that I was at school, any school, yet had not been to my classes for months and was just stuck in the quad or the cafeteria.

Another recurring issue, which likewise at times was a nightmare, was the fact that in the course of starting businesses and managing other people's businesses, I noticed that legal issues always seemed to arise. Whether it was irate customers, acrimonious former employees, or nanny-state regulatory agencies, there was always a legal problem around every bend, and being a layman, I always felt powerless. Since I like to be in control of my own destiny, and I also saw how much those lawyers were billing per hour, I figured it was time to go in a different direction.

The way this unaccredited correspondence law school-thing works in California is a bit more structured than most people would think, but not very much more. Since there are no set class schedules, and in my case, the same "professor" "taught" every subject, the "school" permits open enrollment, meaning that you can enroll at any time throughout the year. The only real caveat is that the State Bar of California ("Calbar") tracks your progress, and you must complete each year of study in no less than 48 weeks and no greater than 52 weeks. Since the course is theoretically part-time law study, the total program consists of 4 years, not 3, hence permitting the existence of a "4L." This is great, I thought. I only work 12 hours a day anyway, so what's another few of hours a night studying law?

An additional bonus of unaccredited law schooling is the California First Year Law Student's Examination or "Baby Bar," which

BARRIOR

is presumably Calbar's means of ensuring that there truly is some form of legal education actually being espoused, as opposed to a mail-order diploma mill or something of the like. If you don't have to take the Baby Bar or any commensurate examination, which most of you probably don't, consider yourself fortunate. Our lack of an LSAT and American Bar Association ("ABA") accreditation requires us to pass the Baby Bar within three attempts, or none of our legal education beyond 1L counts (for Calbar's purposes). This means that if you pass the Baby Bar within three attempts, then you receive credit for your 1L courses and any courses that you have subsequently taken (2L +). If you pass the Baby Bar after three attempts, say on the fourth attempt, you only receive credit for your 1L courses and no other coursework that you may have done subsequently. While it may not sound like it's too bad of a tradeoff for cheap law school with no real barrier to entry, the harsh reality is that approximately 75 percent of all first-time Baby Bar takers fail.

Speaking of harsh reality, when I embarked on this journey, I did not even know what a "1L" was, or anything else, for that matter, that a "normal" law student knows or does. What I did figure out pretty quickly was that there seemed to be a lot of other new students enrolling in this school, most of which were dropping like flies after a month or so of scintillating home study. I never met any of my classmates personally, or even any professor or staff from the school, for that matter, but then again, I didn't want to. I enrolled in this place because it was cheap, they would accept my junior college course credit, and most of all, it was a path to a Bar Card. Even though I didn't know anything about anything related to law school, I did know that a Juris Doctor from this school, or any other unaccredited law school, *sans* Bar Card, would not be worth the paper it was printed on.

It is lonely when you are a correspondence law student, particularly if you ostracize yourself from the chat lectures and school message boards. There are no peers or study groups, no law library, and a continual sense of doubt as to the viability of the whole endeavor. Fortunately for me, the general counsel of the company where I worked, before it imploded in insolvency, had an office adjacent to mine, and aside from being a cerebral guy, he was really cool as well. In talking to him, I realized that he had studied the same courses and many of the same cases as me at his traditional law school, so I figured that at a minimum, my assigned curriculum was not circumspect. I also felt a little bit better about this whole ordeal when I first told him that I had enrolled in a correspondence law school and he didn't respond by laughing in my face. Rather, his first comment was "Wow, that must be hard."

I would guess that the first year of law school, any law school, is hard on most students. I would say that I was personally managing everything pretty well, until things got a little more complicated.

When the bankruptcy of this company occurred and I lost my job, I can't say that I was upset (about losing my job). In reality, I wanted to keep studying law so that I could get my Bar Card, and my biggest concern was how to work that out. My mortgage wasn't going to pay itself, and I was a 35-year-old junior college dropout with a few months of law study at a school that was one notch above clown college. Oh yeah, this was also at a time when the housing bubble burst, the banks and automakers needed a bailout, and unemployment hit double digits.

The last time I went to the office to clean out my desk, my now former boss asked me if I was going to keep up with law school. "Why wouldn't I?" I said. I'm not sure how my response came across, but I subsequently found out from Calbar that they had sent him multiple reference requests related to my Application for Determination of Moral Character, and that he had never responded. When I contacted him about this, he told me that he had been receiving them and had been throwing them away.

After the initial sting of being unemployed wore off, I considered my options, and realizing that they were few and far between, decided to again start my own business. Maybe I wouldn't be sleeping on top of two telemarketing workstations and showering at the gym, but then again, I would need to finish my 1L courses and pass the Baby Bar, all while trying to pull a new business venture out of my hat.

If you are starting to wonder what any of this has to do with you, I'll tell you.

As has become readily apparent, the difference between my formal education and a bucket of crap is the bucket.

If you are a student or graduate of a traditional law school, then you have completed your bachelor's degree, have passed the LSAT, and are studying law with real professors at a real campus. Oh yeah, you are most likely doing this on a full-time basis and over a span of only 3 years, not 4. Ergo, your formal education is far superior to mine.

If you are a student or graduate of an unaccredited correspondence law school, I was right down in the dumps with you, so your formal education is likely no worse than mine.

The bottom line is this: I passed the hardest Bar Examination in the country on the first attempt!

I took the CBX at age forty. If you are younger, in theory anyway, you should be more agile and energetic with a greater aptitude for intellectual pursuits. If you are older than forty, it doesn't matter, since it is all downhill after forty anyway.

Either way, I passed the hardest Bar Examination in the country on the first attempt!

If you lost your job, so did I. If you had a baby, I started a business from scratch after losing my career. If you broke up with your boyfriend, I had to get ready for the Baby Bar while starting said business and trying to keep my head above water as a 2L. We can go on forever, tit-for-tat, with the actual or perceived obstacles, but in spite of life, I passed the hardest Bar Examination in the country on the first attempt!

If life gives you lemons, sell them at pure profit and buy some oranges. Quit making excuses, candidate! I did it, and so can you!

I of the Tiger

IN THE CONTEXT of this book, there are only two things that are important regarding my law school education. First, as we have already established, your law school education is either far superior or no worse. Second, I kept my eye on the prize, always thinking about passing the CBX and getting my Bar Card.

Always keeping my eye on the prize meant that I would have to pass the Baby Bar within three attempts or be forced to redo any courses beyond 1L, assuming, that is, that I passed it during some subsequent attempt. By extrapolation, this meant that not only the 2L and maybe 3L courses would be absolutely worthless without a successful passage of the Baby Bar in three tries, but also that the entire correspondence endeavor would be absolutely worthless given that eventuality. There was just no way in hell that I would redo a year or more of law school, and obviously if it came to that point where I couldn't pass the Baby Bar in three attempts, there was no realistic shot of me ever passing the CBX.

The Baby Bar then became my primary focus at the onset. Essentially, I wanted to pass the Baby Bar more than I wanted to get the best grades in my courses or to become teacher's pet with my professor. That's right, *professor*, singular, as in one dude for the entire 4 years of law school.

Now, had I been younger and gone to a traditional law school, graduating summa cum laude or making the Order of the Coif may have been of interest to me. I point that out since I am not necessarily suggesting that you should abandon any academic goals that you may have in favor of passing the Baby Bar or Bar Examination. This is simply what made the most sense for me based on my particular situation.

When I took my midterms during my 1L year, I did so closed book and in 1 hour per essay, just as I would be required to do so on the

Baby Bar. The midterms at my school actually permitted open book and as much time as required, and, since I was still a 1L, I could have used them both. However, having my eye on the prize, I unilaterally decided to mimic the Baby Bar. I didn't do that well on the midterms, but I didn't well care either.

When I took my finals during my 1L year, I did so closed book and in 3 hours, or 1 hour per essay, just as I would be required to do so on the Baby Bar. The finals at my school were required to be closed book and proctored, yet, there were up to 3 days to take all of the tests. I was still a 1L and probably could have used the extra time. However, having my eye on the prize, I decided to mimic the Baby Bar. I didn't do that poorly on the finals, but I didn't well care either.

Having received mediocre grades as a 1L, I was permitted to pass "go" and begin my 2L courses. However, I had the Baby Bar coming up in approximately 4 months, and again, I had to pass this SOB or else. While three attempts was the line in the sand that Calbar had determined as the breaking point, I had a different idea—one-and-done, son. No coming back, no "better luck next time," no "what's important is how you play the game."

I paid my 2L course tuition, bought my 2L books, did the bare minimum in terms of my 2L assignments and required work, and essentially focused all of my time and energy on preparing for the Baby Bar. I knew that if I passed the Baby Bar on the first attempt, which as I mentioned, only about 25 percent of candidates do, the loss of 3 months of 2L study would make the courses more difficult and ultimately would affect my grades. Then again, I also knew that if I failed the Baby Bar on the first attempt, I would have to take it again, which would, in turn, cause me to lose another 3 months of 2L study, making the courses even more difficult and ultimately affecting my grades even more. If I didn't pass the Baby Bar after two attempts, the 2L year would be of no educational value, assuming I passed it, since all of my time would be focused on taking and then retaking the Baby Bar.

After I passed the Baby Bar on the first attempt, I remember feeling vindicated to a certain degree about what I was doing with this correspondence law stuff. If you go to a traditional law school, then you likely don't know what I'm referring to, but if you go to a correspondence law school, then you probably can relate.

The truth is that when you are teaching yourself the law in your boxers at 3:00 a.m., the process seems surreal at best, almost like it's a farce or something. When you take and pass a candidate killer like the Baby Bar on the first attempt, you start to feel like you are not just wasting your time and your money after all, but rather, have learned, and are learning, the law. Passing the Baby Bar was, for me, the equivalent of law school legitimization.

I also remember feeling that the focus would now need to turn to the CBX, even though that examination was still in the distant future. Using the same plan of attack that I had employed in anticipation of the Baby Bar, I spent the rest of my law school experience doing my midterms and finals under CBX-like conditions, and likewise, I began to use the same techniques I had learned in Baby Bar review to nail my law school courses and make my gradual ascent toward the CBX. I have dedicated additional chapters to address with more specificity what exactly I did to prepare for the Baby Bar and the CBX (and even law school). What is therefore important here is that you realize my perspective at the time so that you can assess your own perspective at this time.

Given the possible ramifications of a Baby Bar failure, I made the necessary adjustments to my priorities in order to ensure myself the best possible chance for first-time success. First-time success to me translated into one hurdle less on the track to the Bar Card. Sure, it was risky to create added conditions to my law school examinations. Sure, it was risky to double-down on my 1L studies while technically enrolled in my 2L courses. Sure, it was risky to care less about being in good graces with my one and only professor.

Sure, but my assessment was that the reward for me far outweighed any such risk.

Ask yourself, then, what it is that you need to change or rearrange, if anything. Are your priorities conducive to passing the Baby Bar or Bar Examination, or are your focus and energy directed elsewhere?

After you pass the Bar Examination, there is an oath that you must take as a requisite to being admitted to practice law. While the pomp and circumstance ceremony is not required, as there are other ways to take the oath, I personally wanted to participate in the ceremony in order to add some normality to an otherwise abnormal legal education.

At this ceremony, there were some representatives present from Calbar as well as some California Superior Court and Federal District Court magistrates. Some even addressed the audience. While the totality of the comments and advice bestowed upon us in attendance was sage and pithy, there is one bit of advice in particular that I will never forget. You should never forget it either.

"As new lawyers about to embark on your chosen profession, you are afraid of what's out there. I was afraid too, and so were all of the judges behind me when they were new lawyers. In fact, we are all still afraid today. But don't let the fear stop you. Take risks; take risks."

Stay thirsty, my friend. Take risks.

Certified Law Jerk

BY THE TIME I became a 3L, I decided to seek out a legal internship. While I have never liked the idea of working without pay, and, in fact, am philosophically opposed to it, I realized that I was studying law in a vacuum and wanted to get a better perspective of what being a lawyer is really like. Some law students do it for extra course credit, others to line up a possible paying associate gig upon passing the Bar Examination, and still others because they feel obligated to do it. Some don't do it at all.

When I passed the Baby Bar and began taking certain courses prescribed by Calbar, I became eligible for Calbar certification as a Certified Law Clerk or Certified Law Student, depending on whatever the nomenclature was at the time. These titles were basically euphemisms for a minimally competent law student who would work for free under a lawyer's supervision.

Since my law school was located somewhere in cyberspace, and there were probably very few lawyers that they had ever graduated, there was no network, no bulletin board, and no offers for internships from any law firms. This meant that if I wanted an internship, I was going to have to find it myself, so I began applying to classified ads, most of which were seeking a paralegal or a lackey or a combination thereof, none of which ever responded to my résumé. I then decided to place my own classified ad looking for a lawyer that wanted an intern. I got a call that very same day.

The "lawyer" that called me claimed to have an office in an upscale part of the county, and by all accounts seemed to have a lot of experience and a successful family law practice. We spoke on the phone for nearly an hour, at which time he told me that he would "hire" me without a formal interview, given that I had impressed him during our phone conversation. *First warning sign.* He then asked me if I could start that afternoon. *Second warning sign.*

BARRIOR

I put on a suit and went down to his "office" that afternoon. When I pulled up, I thought I must have written down the address wrong. While the location was proximate to the beach and multimillion-dollar homes, it was on the second story of a Class D strip mall, the anchor tenant, of which, was a liquor store. *Third warning sign.* I was seriously thinking about not stopping and just driving home, and in retrospect, I wish that I would have.

As I walked in, there was a door chime or something but no receptionist at the front desk. I could hear a person or two in the back, and they had to have seen me walk by their windows in order to enter this dump, but nevertheless, nobody came out to greet me. I coughed, cleared my throat, and rifled through a couple of magazines, but still no reception.

When I showed myself in, it looked like that boiler room I worked at for 2 hours probably looked after it had been raided. There were literally file boxes, documents, and all kinds of junk all over the place, just no people. I then looked to my left, and inside of a shoebox office was some gangly looking fool who was trying to act like he didn't know I was there. *I ran out of warning signs and am now driving off of a cliff.*

Trying to be professional and lawyerlike in this most unprofessional and litter boxlike place, I introduced myself and said that I was the law clerk that was supposed to start working today. Rather than introduce himself back, this guy got up and said, "Oh yeah, so-and-so told me you were coming. He wants you to print out these letters, and then get them ready for mailing."

I was led into an even worse office with furniture from the bus station and a computer that might as well have been an abacus. My new friend here, who I think was a lawyer, showed me where this letter file was located, and then left. When I started printing out the letters, I realized that this family law practice was really something akin to a marketing mill seeking out women for possible egg donation and or surrogate mother opportunities. I also realized that the phone seemed to be ringing off the hook in this place, yet nobody seemed interested in answering it.

Since the lawyer that I had spoken with on the phone was not yet there, I figured I would stuff some of these envelopes until he arrived, and then, hopefully, get a chance to speak with him in greater detail regarding what the internship would entail, possibilities to draft motions, court appearances, and the like. After a couple of hours, I heard someone else in there and could sense that somebody was watching me, but nobody ever came in or spoke with me. After about a half hour of this, I headed to the restroom at the end of the hall, and upon exiting, saw a portly, bald man with a clownlike tie standing by the copy machine, looking at me. I said "hello," not knowing if this was a lawyer or a client or a carnival barker, to which he said, "hello." I remember thinking that I had seen this guy somewhere before, but I couldn't put a finger on it.

"Are you Tim?" he asked me. *No shit* I was thinking to myself.

"Yes, and you must be attorney so-and-so?"

"Yes, that's me."

After the exchange of pleasantries, I could tell that he was not interested in talking more about my future plans or even what his "firm" could offer me in terms of legal experience in exchange for my servitude. Instead, he asked me if I had seen the other file of letters that should have gone out 3 months ago but never did.

When I was sitting there printing these letters and stuffing envelopes for free, I was really tempted to go to the liquor store downstairs, grab a 40 ounce, conceal it in a brown paper bag, and walk down to the beach. I figured that I had wasted my day already, and there was no experience to be gained by slaving away for this putz. That was about the time that he came in to the office and showed me a picture of a good-looking woman with a nice body, followed by a very professionally responsible "This is one of the women that responded to my ad seeking egg donors. I'd fertilize her!" *Not with that tie, you won't,* I was thinking to myself.

I actually finished out the pile of letters before taking off, because that's just me. Lawyer so-and-so asked me what schedule I was thinking about working going forward, and I told him that I would get back to him since I had to figure out what days were best, since, after all, I was also running my own company and studying law at the time. The truth is that I had already made up my mind never to return, in part, because of the laughingstock of a practice that this guy was running, and in part, because I looked him up on the Web (from my phone) to see if I could figure out why he looked so familiar.

As it turns out, lawyer so-and-so had been on the local news several times in response to a myriad of client complaints regarding just about every ethical violation you can think of. There was even a video of a "gotcha" news crew entering his office to speak with him about some of these allegations. The video showed some petrified law clerks or staff that was unfortunate to have been present when the whole thing went down, which is, undoubtedly, why he needed to bring in some new, unwitting, intern blood. He was even wearing that same tie in the video.

If you think that's funny, about a month later and having never returned nor speaking to him again, he emailed me to ask if I had decided on my internship schedule yet (with his firm).

When I read his order for disbarment it sounded like a Bar Examination hypothetical on steroids; Unauthorized practice, moral turpitude (three counts), illegal fees, failure to respond to client inquiries, failure to deposit client funds in trust accounts (two counts), failure to refund unearned fees (four counts), failure to render accounts of client funds (two counts), unconscionable fees, failure to release files and failure to comply with conditions of probation. Yes, probation, as in he had been previously disciplined and still didn't get it together.

He had also previously been arrested for allegedly attempting to hire someone to murder his estranged wife, and, as of this writing, has been charged with theft in relation to a scheme to allegedly collect rents from apartments, apartments which he does not own.

A little bit fazed by all of this, I kept placing my classified ad and eventually I got another couple of hits. One came from a criminal defense lawyer downtown, and a perusal of his website led me to believe that he was, in fact, running a real law practice. I called him, and we set up an appointment down at his office a couple of days later.

The place was quaint, and there was also no receptionist, but this Attorney greeted me right away. He didn't put me to work that very instant answering his phones or sending out past-due mailings, but instead, started talking to me about his practice, his experience, and my particular legal goals and objectives. He then showed me a graphic photograph from a sexual abuse case that he was defending and asked me if I could handle it since he had apparently worked with a lot of interns in the past that did not have the stomach for it. "Looks like a regular Saturday night for me," I responded in a flippant manner.

"Great, when can you start?" he asked.

Day one was a trip to the courthouse to observe a Felony Readiness Conference in some counterfeit money case. Day two, and most subsequent days, was rife with more courthouse trips, jail visits, and a peppering of research and motion writing in between. In most instances, the courthouse visits and motions were not just me observing, but me actually appearing under his supervision.

Being that I was Certified, Attorney decided to throw me into the fire the first week to see how badly I would get burned. The first time, in a morning hearing, things went off without a hitch. Later that afternoon, in another hearing, I got my ass handed to me by a crotchety old judge. I didn't know what I was doing, and really what I should say, but he could have been more diplomatic about it. When Attorney attempted to chime in, the judge screamed, "Who is the lawyer here? Are you the lawyer or is he the lawyer?" That was really embarrassing, but at least we (he) won the motion for the client.

Most of what I did before the court went off without a hitch, and I was really enjoying this lawyering stuff. In fact, I began to enjoy it so much that I was starting to do all kinds of work around the place, sitting at the defense table every day for weeks at a time during trials and oftentimes would put in anywhere from 10–12 hours a day, without pay. Even worse, this was 10–12 hours per day that I needed for running my own company, as well as studying.

Right before I graduated as a 4L, I actually litigated a criminal trial, again, under the supervision of Attorney. I had met the client, the defendant, when I participated in the original intake interview as a translator, since the client did not speak English, and I (now) speak Spanish fluently. Surprisingly, even though I had only done some translating, the client didn't have a problem letting me, a law student, try his case. Cool.

On the morning of trial, Attorney had to run to another courthouse in the county to deal with another client's issue. He therefore instructed me to go to the Trial Setting Department and notify the prosecutor that he would be there shortly.

I had not met the prosecutor prior to the day of trial. He was a younger guy with a friendly demeanor, and he had no problem in trailing the matter until Attorney could arrive. After about an hour, Attorney called me and told me to ask the bailiff to inform the judge that he would be there within a half hour.

When I approached the bailiff, wearing a suit and carrying a briefcase, he asked me for the case name. I gave it to him, but before I could say that the attorney of record, Attorney, would be there in less than half an hour, the bailiff started to approach the clerk, I'm guessing as a means of locating the file. When the judge saw the bailiff approaching the clerk, he asked the bailiff what the case name was. When the bailiff told him, the judge blurted out "Who are *you*?" I had been in this judge's courtroom several times along with Attorney, so he already knew that I was a law clerk.

"Good morning, Your Honor. Timothy Miranda, Certified Law Clerk. I was just attempting to tell the bai—"

"A law clerk practicing law without supervision?" he screamed.

"Well, Your Honor, technically I wasn't pract—"

"You can be reported to the State Bar for the unauthorized practice of law for being up here outside of the presence of a supervising attorney," he screamed again.

"I understand, Your Honor, but I wasn't pract—"

"So if I were you, I wouldn't stand in front of this court any longer than I had to. Instead, I would take this opportunity to get out of here right now before I got myself into trouble."

"Yes, Your Honor," I said as I walked out of there with my briefcase between my legs. This department was the first stop for most felony matters, and it was a busy morning in there, packed with some of the most prominent criminal defense lawyers in town and bunch of other, less prominent people in the audience. What an inauspicious beginning to my first trial, but then again, I served myself up on a silver platter. The fact is that if you are a law clerk, you are always subject to a judge's berating without notice. By going up there, I gave him a shot, and he took it.

As for the trial, after voir dire, things got off to a decent start. Since this was a criminal trial, the prosecutor bore the burden of proof and, likewise, had to go first. When the prosecutor would conduct direct examination of a witness, sometimes I would object by myself, sometimes I would miss an objection and Attorney would chime in, and sometimes we would object in unison. I have to give credit to the judge, as she was very accommodating.

When it was my turn to cross-examine the first witness, a police officer, I wasn't at my best. I had cross-examined police officers before during motions to suppress evidence and the like, but in a trial, with a jury, it is different. Fortunately, at the end of my cross-examination, it was too late in the day for the prosecutor to call another witness, so I was granted a temporary reprieve until the next day.

Attorney, seeing that I wasn't at my best, told me to just relax. He said that I looked uncomfortable, as if I was overanalyzing my questions, and he even offered to take over if I felt like I couldn't handle this. Attorney is a seasoned litigator who has spent most of the past two decades in court. Not pushing papers, not playing golf, but doing trials. I knew if Attorney said it, then he was right. I settled down, followed his lead, and got into a groove. Ultimately, I shredded all of the prosecution's witnesses.

BARRIOR

My client was an elderly "greeter" who had worked at a major retail establishment. The alleged victim was about half his age and had been a customer of this major retail establishment. When my client attempted to check the receipt of the alleged victim as he exited, the alleged victim had other ideas. There was security video of this whole ordeal as you might expect, and the prosecutor construed it in favor of the alleged victim, charging my client with assault and battery. Not only was my client elderly, but he was overweight, walked with a limp, and had a voice like a schoolchild.

You know I put him on the stand for the jury to see and hear.

When closing argument came due, one of the ill-fated statements that the prosecutor made, while trying to be jocular, was that my client was the initial aggressor and had taken a swing at the alleged victim but had missed. "A swing and a miss," he said. When I gave my closing argument, I mockingly continued forward with his baseball analogy.

"Ladies and gentlemen, you heard the prosecutor characterize, or rather mischaracterize, that defensive brush-off you saw on the security video as a 'swing and a miss.' Paradoxically, in baseball, a swing and a miss is what? It's a strike. However, in a court of law, a strike, or a battery, cannot be a swing and a miss, but rather *must* be a swing and a hit. Not only was there not even a swing, so no assault, but as the prosecutor just told you, there was no hit either. If this were a baseball game, the indictment might have some merit, but according to the laws of this state, there cannot be an assault or a battery."

After about 45 minutes of waiting out in the hall, the clerk informed us that the jury had reached a verdict. Not guilty on all counts.

What started off as a kick in the nuts in Trial Setting, compounded by an initial lackluster cross-examination, had an otherwise happy ending. Coincidentally, it was my birthday, but the verdict was not a gift. I spent a lot of time going over the discovery, making my notes and practicing my closing argument in front of the mirror. I watched that security video so many times that I actually knew the number of tiles on the floor.

The jury gave me accolades. The judge told me that I did an excellent job, and even the bailiff told me that he would hire me if he ever needed a lawyer. *This is better than sex,* I thought. Almost.

For me, the internship was a great way to get some practical experience, to meet other lawyers, and to see just what the profession is really all about. From a law school or Bar Examination point of view, the writing of motions and, in my case, involvement with criminal matters, really helped make subjects like Constitutional Law, Criminal Law, Criminal Procedure and Evidence much more interesting and user friendly.

In sum, I believe this was good experience that ultimately helped me pass the CBX, in particular, when I would get the Multistate Bar Examination ("MBE") questions related to these very subjects. If you do a trial, it is hard to miss an MBE question about a trial.

If you can swing an internship in the midst of all your studying, then swing it. Just be sure to avoid the swing and a miss.

> "Nobody ever defended anything successfully; there is only attack and attack and attack some more."
> —*General George S. Patton*

I'll Take 2

MOST TRADITIONAL LAW schools are full-time, 3-year programs that graduate their students in May. As a result, many of these students (candidates) opt to sit for their first eligible Bar Examination in July. I graduated around the same time of the year myself, and theoretically was eligible to sit for the July examination. Notwithstanding, I chose to take it in February instead.

If you are a student of the Bar Examination like I was and not just a student that studies for the Bar Examination, you realize that the February administration tends to have fewer applicants, and that those applicants tend to have a harder time passing. Depending on whom you ask, this is due to the fact that the questions are harder and or the candidate pool is rife with repeaters that failed in July (or is even tainted by open enrollment graduates from unaccredited correspondence schools, such as myself). Regardless of the reason, the pass rates are markedly lower in February, and as such, most candidates feel compelled to sit in July to avoid the wrath of February.

When I graduated, my knee-jerk reaction was to sit for the July CBX as well. After all, it had been 4 long years of law school for me, and my indoctrination into the world of lawyering as an intern had really made me even more eager to get my Bar Card. Nevertheless, I ultimately opted to sit for the February examination, meaning that nearly 5 years had transpired from the time that I enrolled in law school to the time that I actually sat for the CBX.

In spite of the advice and support of my friends and family, this was a decision that was mine alone to make. After all, I had been the one that had had to endure (and pay for) law school and likewise would be the only one that had to sit for the examination. I was certainly conflicted, but ultimately followed my gut. For me, things usually work out better when I follow my gut.

Everything is relative, and had I been knee-deep in student loans or had a choice associate position waiting for me upon my successful passage of the July CBX, I might have chosen otherwise. While I didn't have these pressures, I had other pressures that were influencing my decision. Principally, I just didn't feel like I was ready to go in there and give it my best. Maybe it was the fact that law school for me was so drawn out. Maybe it was the fact that I spent too much time interning in my last 2 years of law school, or maybe I just didn't feel like it. Maybe you just don't feel like it either.

Instead, the weekend before the July CBX that year, I went to Las Vegas and had a great time, except for the fact that I couldn't help but feeling guilty that I wasn't studying only a couple of days before the examination. On the following Tuesday, the first day of the examination, I felt guilty again. This time I felt guilty that I wasn't there taking it. These feelings were compounded by the sentiments of well-wishing friends who continued to tell me that I should have sat because I would have passed. Could've, should've, would've.

Once the July CBX was over that Thursday afternoon I felt like a weight had been lifted from my shoulders, as now the next, and only, CBX that I could sit for was the forthcoming February examination. At this point, it was nearly 7 months away, but it actually felt good to be back in the saddle, and this time I was starting to "feel like it."

By the time I sat for the examination, I had been the beneficiary of a lengthy yet well-planned and well-executed Bar study regimen. Not only did I have my law down cold, but I also had a good degree of confidence and a general feeling that I was ready to not only take, but pass the CBX on the first attempt. That preparation paired with confidence is why I passed.

Ironically, my confidence was also derived from the fact that, statistically speaking, the February CBX is more difficult to pass than the July CBX. Where most candidates see crisis, I saw opportunity.

With fewer applicants, I figured that the venue would likewise be smaller in scale and thus, not be so noisy, crowded, or oppressive to someone who is getting ready to take the test of their life. Being that the examination was in February, I knew that I would need to forsake some holiday cheer in late December due to studying, which was unfortunate because I had these really sensational ski poles to break in. Conversely and fortunately, my office would be closed for the holidays, and this would mean that I would have much less distractions. Studying during the winter is not that much different than studying during the summer when you live in Southern California, but for me, it always seemed easier to study in the winter than in the summer, when all I could think about was getting outdoors.

Then, of course, there were these tougher questions on the February examination that always seemed to claim more victims than in July. While this was a common misconception of my Bar candidate brethren, I knew it to be a fallacy. I knew this since, as I have already mentioned, I had studied the CBX, not just studied for it, and realized that there really were no differences between the February and July administrations.

MBE questions are, for the most part, a combination of repeat questions and similar fact pattern questions with different names, dates, or whatever they do to attempt to cloak it, making the test virtually the same during each and every administration. If it is more difficult or easier than the previous administration, the scaling, or equating, is supposed to give you the same net result.

Former essay questions for the CBX are available everywhere, and since I wrote them and reviewed them, ad nauseam, I never detected a difference in difficulty between the two different test administrations. While the essay subjects are variable, I was also predicting my essays and, thus, had a pretty good idea of what to expect.

Performance Tests ("PTs") are PTs; same crap, different examination. One is usually a memo or a letter, and the other is usually a Points and Authorities type of test. One PT is usually harder than the other one, and one PT is usually easier than the other one.

If it's not the curriculum, it must be the candidates.

Based on the CBX statistics, the unaccredited correspondence students like me have a far worse percentage of first-time passage on the examination. We are talking percentages in the teens at best, and the repeaters, from any type of school, usually don't get above 30 percent. To me, this was a good thing.

My logic was quite simple; if the candidate pool is generally weak, my work product should then stand out in the crowd, demonstrating to the graders that I know my law, know how to write, put in the work, and deserve a Bar Card. Fortunately the graders were all in accord.

As for you, this is where the introspection comes in to play once again. Based on your set of circumstances, your feelings and your objectives, what is the right choice for you? "For you" is the operative phrase, as ultimately, you are the only one that will have to endure the long months of study and even longer months of post-Bar examination waiting.

> Johnny Ringo: "You wretched slugs. Don't any of you have the guts to play for blood?"
> Doc Holliday: "I'm your huckleberry. That's *just* my game."
> —*Tombstone* (1993)

Beginner Schmuck

LUCK, OR LACK thereof, is an issue often discussed by examination repeaters in the context of why they were not successful on the Baby Bar or Bar Examination, and moreover, why their passing candidate compatriots were, in fact, successful. A repeater will often claim that they were unlucky to receive a low score because they got a grader that was in a bad mood that day, or the grader didn't even read their essay or PT answer completely because they only make a couple of bucks per. Likewise, the contention of misfortune may be based upon the fact one or two of the essays were on a subject that the candidate is not proficient at, and had the essays been on any other subject, they would have passed the examination. This is a total fallacy employed by those who fail in order to rationalize or excuse a piss-poor performance! There simply is no excuse for failing by a few points, and to bring luck into the equation is an insult to luck.

No matter how you stack it, what permits a candidate to pass the examination is hard, smart work. A by-product of this is the ability to enter the testing center with the confidence that there is nothing that the Committee of Bar Examiners ("Bar Examiners") can throw at you that you have not seen before. When you have this level of confidence, the examination is the one that is unlucky.

If you accidentally input an MBE answer on the wrong, noncorresponding numbered space on your answer sheet, and therefore all of your subsequent answers are likewise on the wrong, noncorresponding numbered space on your answer sheet, are you unlucky that you missed twenty-five questions in a row? Or, are you just a careless candidate that didn't take the time to verify some of your answers to make sure that the questions and answers were matching up correctly? If you run out of time with 10 questions left, are you unlucky, or did you just not do enough practice MBEs under timed conditions to figure out how to get your internal clock dialed-in? Was I unlucky when I started out getting only 50 percent or so of my MBEs correct in practice, and then lucky when I consistently got nearly 90 percent of them correct?

If your PTs are two memo-type questions instead of one memo and one Points and Authorities-type question, and typically you do better on the Points and Authorities variety, is this bad luck or simply a plausible outcome that should have been accounted for by you during your review regimen? I was probably one of the lowest-scoring PT takers on my CBX, not because of the examination itself, or the luck of the draw, but rather, because I was just no good at them. No excuses, no sugarcoating here.

On day two, I got a Points and Authorities fact pattern, the ones I liked the least, and to compound my disgust, the subject matter was totally foreign to me (literally). Rather than Torts or Criminal Procedure or anything that I had taken in law school and which I at least knew something about, the fact pattern was that of a foreign immigrant seeking asylum, better known as Immigration Law. Was I unlucky because I happened to get a subject that I had no knowledge of, and in the Points and Authorities format which I hated? No, because I practiced enough to anticipate a worst-case scenario and simply decided to take control of my own destiny and write the hell out of that exam, even though I never really understood it. I was tired, it was the last exam on the last day, and I was lost and confused, but I kept slugging, refusing to succumb to a grade of 40. Always pick yourself up off of the canvas and keep slugging.

Essays are where the luck card is played the most often, usually by a candidate that compares the essay subjects of some former Baby Bar or Bar Examination to those of the examination that they sat for and failed. In the alternative, the comparison is made by a candidate looking at the essays of the Baby Bar or Bar Examination just administered prior to their own, forthcoming examination, and thinking, "Wow, I wish I could have gotten *those* essays." I was eligible to sit in July, and I'll admit that when I saw the essays that were administered on that examination, I remember having this inclination myself. But this inclination for me quickly turned in to a feeling of needing to get busy, ready to hit whatever they pitched to me in February.

On this note, as you'll see, I ended up predicting most of the essay subjects that appeared on my examination, both for the Baby Bar and the CBX. Does this prescient ability make me lucky, or does it merely make the time that I spent in trying to predict my poison seem like a worthwhile investment?

Lucky is for the lottery and 2:00 a.m. on a Saturday night; unlucky is for getting hit by lightning. Passing the Bar Examination is all about hard, smart work, kicking ass with no use for taking names, and walking out of that testing center knowing you will never be back. Like I said, one-and-done, son.

> "I believe in luck. And the harder I work, the luckier I get."
> —Dan Gable, 1972 Olympic Gold Medal Winner
> (Wrestling)

Bar Revue

A: SHOULD YOU spend thousands of dollars on a Bar review course, and B: If so, which one? Yes. And, I don't know.

Whether you are going to sit for the Baby Bar or Bar Examination, a review course is of paramount importance if you never want to sit again. With so much potential subject matter to cover, and with all of the potential topics contained within the subjects to cover, a focused, condensed approach is simply indispensible. Additionally, depending upon when and where you learned certain subjects in law school, it is possible that the law has since changed or is even different.

In regards to which review course to select, I can only be of limited assistance here. You see, I used the same company for both my Baby Bar and CBX review, Fleming's Fundamentals of Law ("Fleming's"), and while I thought both review courses were excellent, I don't have any empirical data by which to compare and contrast their programs against those of other companies. Sure, I could read the forums and message boards on the law student websites and adopt the opinions of candidates that have used other companies, but if they have used other companies and are posting about it, chances are they failed the examination (or they would be on to bigger and better things).

If they failed the examination, was it really the fault of the review course that they used, or the faulty way that they used the review course?

What I can tell you is that any review course worth its salt should provide you with a complete review that encompasses all aspects of your respective examination. MBEs, essays, PTs, or whatever is on your Baby Bar or Bar Examination should be included in your review course and materials.

For the Baby Bar, Fleming's provided a robust number of MBE questions from their own book, *Fleming's Fundamentals of Law Multistate Examination Workbook*, and likewise, a book entitled

Strategies and Tactics for the Finz Multistate Method, along with a series of key questions to be taken in this book. There were also some Contracts, Criminal Law, and Torts MBE questions from PMBR that were included. As for the essay portion of the Baby Bar, Fleming's included hundreds of former, actual Baby Bar essay questions, including oftentimes a candidate's sample answer along with their actual Baby Bar grade.

For the CBX, Fleming's provided MBE questions from their own book and the Finz book again, as well as thousands of former MBE questions which had been released by the National Committee of Bar Examiners ("NCBE"). The essay questions were comprised of hundreds of former, actual CBX questions going all the way back to the 1970s, and most included a candidate's sample answer. As for the PTs, there was an entirely separate review dedicated to this alone, which likewise included former, actual CBX questions and some candidate answers with their actual CBX grade.

Aside from all of the materials provided for both the Baby Bar and CBX review courses, there were hours of comprehensive lecture on both the law and the strategies required to do well on each component of the examination.

Since I was a self-taught candidate from the onset, I saw no need to go and take Baby Bar or Bar review courses with other candidates in a live setting. Rather, I chose to purchase a home study review course for both examinations and do the work on my own schedule. I also wanted to avoid the distractions, chatter, and even more important, have a tangible set of review materials that I could continue to return to in the event I didn't fully understand the subject or topic. I'm sure that if you go and take the course live you get all of the books and handouts, but then again, the lecture is live and only lasts once. If you receive recorded lectures, you can keep referring back to them as necessary.

If I had contemporaries from law school it probably would have been more pleasant to take a live course and continue to propagate my collegiate friendships and social network. Then again, I might have focused too much on my friendships and social networking and not paid enough attention to the lectures.

Do some comparison shopping, see what the companies have to offer you, and determine whether it is a good fit for you and your own specific needs, jurisdictional requirements, and or budget. Look to what the price includes, and whether you will need to purchase additional materials outside of what is included with the review course. Above all, keep in mind that paying for the review course is actually the easy part.

Just add hustle.

The Art of Bar

Each jurisdiction has their own respective minimum passing score for the Bar Examination. In California, the requisite minimum score to pass the CBX is 1,440 out of 2,000 total points, while the Baby Bar requires a minimum passing score of 560 out of 800 points. Hopefully from the outset you will adopt the glass half-full mentality and realize that you can miss a lot of points on either examination and still pass it. No matter how you look at it, the Bar Examiners like to call this "minimal competency."

Given that examination scoring varies by jurisdiction, and likewise, is always subject to change, you should always begin by ascertaining exactly what the current scoring calculus is for your particular examination. With that said, at present, the Baby Bar gives equivalent weight to both the MBEs and the essays, with each contributing a respective 50 percent of the total score.

On the CBX, the MBE questions comprise 35 percent of the total score, while the essays comprise 39 percent of the total score. The PTs pack the least amount of punch of the three, comprising only 26 percent of the total score. Since there are two PTs, each respective score is counted twice, for a total of four scores. The essay scores, six in total, are only counted once, just like the MBEs. Here is a quick visual:

MBE Score + Essay 1 + Essay 2 + Essay 3 + Essay 4 + Essay 5 + Essay 6 + PT 1 + PT 1 + PT 2 + PT 2

Whatever your raw score is on each component, MBE, essay, and PT, it is then scaled or equated, a process which is fluid (and which will never truly be understood by mere mortals). You really need not concern yourself with it either, as the scaled score is merely a derivative of the raw score you put forth. So concern yourself instead with putting forth a high raw score.

◄ BARRIOR

With its three testing components, think of the CBX as a three-headed monster. If you were to ever see a three-headed monster in real life, it would probably scare the hell out of you, which is exactly what the Bar Examiners had in mind. Minimal competency begins with pruning out those candidates that are not cut from the right cloth to be a lawyer, such as those who are meek, easily intimidated, lack confidence, or are otherwise unable to deal with incessant stress and pressure. Some candidates never even sit for the exam, some leave the jurisdiction in search of an easier Bar Examination, and some just keep failing.

Ironically however, the size and scope of an examination such as the CBX is what, in fact, makes it passable.

The easiest way to peel back the layers is to break the test down into its three components and assign each component roughly a one-third point contribution value. Under this type of simplified analysis, you can generally be weaker in one component and still pass the CBX if you are stronger in the other two components.

Obviously, the six essays on the CBX are worth more, apples-to-apples, than either the MBEs or the PTs. This means that if you are stronger on the essays, you can make up for one other weaker component, and possibly even a little more weakness in another component. In the alternative, since there are six essays in total, if you can get good scores on at least three of them, you can likely survive two mediocre scores and one poor score on the other three essays, and still get out of the essays with enough points to make up for one other weaker component. Conversely, if you are weak at the essays, you would need a stellar performance in the other two components to pass.

MBEs on the CBX are worth less than the six essays but more than the PTs. Therefore, ideally, if you are stronger on the MBE and need to use these scores to compensate for another, weaker component, it should be the PTs and not the essays. However, if of the six essays only two were poor, a good MBE score might still serve to compensate. "Might" is the operative word.

If you are stronger on PTs, the fact that they are the component that contributes the lowest point value means that while they will take some pressure off of the other two components, on a one-to-one basis they are not enough to make up for a weaker area. If you are stronger on PTs, you will still need a pretty good essay score and a pretty good MBE score to pass.

Again, the easiest, although not the most precise way to think about all of this is to think of the test as the amalgamation of three components, ascribing each component a one-third point contribution value. Your overarching goal should be strength in two components and moderate, manageable, weakness, if any, in the remaining third component.

I realized early on that I was the strongest on the MBEs and essays, yet poor on the PTs. Again, this was my particular triumvirate, and you may be the opposite; it doesn't matter which witch is which, since the point is that everyone feels better about some components of this examination than others. However, merely realizing what your own strengths and weaknesses are is futile unless you do something about it.

I started by creating a spreadsheet that would allow me to input raw scores for each of the three components, and then scale them in a manner consistent (I hoped) with that of the actual CBX scaling. The scores would then be added together, and if the aggregate were greater than 1,440, I would know that those scores would be enough to pass the examination. The scores that I would input were obviously hypothetical yet not completely out of left field, as each was founded on real data.

The MBE score I would input was based upon my historical percentage of correct answers which I had been tracking since when I first started preparing for the Baby Bar. For example, I might input a best-case scenario of a raw MBE score of 170 or a worst-case scenario of a raw MBE score of 150.

My hypothetical essay scores were based upon several factors, beginning with my essay predictions. Once I had what I believed was a valid prediction of what essay subjects may arise on my forthcoming CBX, I could then approximate the scores based upon how I historically did on those essay subjects. Again, I would input a best-case scenario, giving myself an average of 70–75 on each essay, and likewise, would create a worst-case scenario where I totally bombed at least one essay (50) and received mediocre scores on at least one or two of the others (60–65).

PTs were for me the real variable. Here, my best-case scenario was a 60 or a 65 for one PT and a 50 or a 55 for the other PT, and my worst-case scenario was a 50 and a 40, respectively. If you consider that the essays and PTs are graded on a scale from 40 to 100 points, in increments of 5 points, a 40 was the lowest possible score that could be attained as long as I showed up and wrote something. Even so, with some solid MBE and essay scores, my analysis actually indicated that I could still pass the CBX if I received only a 50 and a 40 on the PTs.

While this might seem like a lot of additional work, that is, predicting, keeping track of your results, and then analyzing everything, I must tell you that it is just as important to your examination preparation as anything else you may do. Again, the premise is that you are taking stock of yourself, determining your own strengths and weaknesses, and then utilizing this information to proactively develop a strategy for success.

As you can see, the MBE and essay scores I input into my analysis were very strong. I knew these scores were strong and yet attainable, not because I read the forums or message boards on the law student websites and listened to what other candidates told me, but rather because I kept my own scorecard and was able to determine what I could usually expect to achieve. The PTs were clearly my Achilles, which I knew because I compared them to the sample or model answers and assigned my own answers a score relative to those sample or model answers. Having this weak PT link in my scoring chain made me very concerned about my prospects of passing the examination, and had I not taken the time to make a strategic analysis of my score, the concern would have snowballed into anxiety and intimidation, and I would have failed the CBX before I ever took it.

Being a (successful) lawyer requires, inter alia, strategy and planning, which is exactly why the Baby Bar and Bar Examination require strategy and planning. A minimally competent lawyer will not take the advice of fools or avoid research and investigation in favor of crossing their fingers or carrying a rabbit's foot in their briefcase.

Use the CBX Score Analyzer at Barrior.com and figure out where you are today and where you need to be in February or July. You will be amazed at how an extra five points in one essay or an extra three correct MBE questions can affect your overall score, and ultimately determine your CBX fate.

The bigger they are, the harder they fall, if you know where to hit them.

Stratustician

SOME JURISDICTIONS, LIKE California, have dismal first-time examination pass rates while other jurisdictions have less dismal first-time pass rates. What is important to realize is that there is never a 100 percent first-time pass rate, nor a 100 percent repeater pass rate, for that matter, anywhere. In other words, there are always some candidates that will pass and always some candidates that will fail.

When I took the Baby Bar, I didn't know a single person that was there. Not only was the venue about 2 hours away from my home, but also the fact that I did a correspondence program meant that I would not know one of my fellow classmates, assuming that there were even any of them there, if they crashed into me in the parking lot. Honestly, this suited me just fine, since the last thing I wanted to do, and the last thing you should ever do, is start jawing about the examination with other candidates. Unfortunately, as the doors to the testing area opened and we were all herded toward our seats, there were a couple of buffoons standing in front of me that just couldn't keep their traps shut immediately prior to what you would think is one of the most important days of their lives.

"This is my second time," said one of them. "Me too," said the other. "That Contracts question was really hard on the last one ... that's why I failed." "Yeah, I got a 40 on it." "Wow, I think they give you a 40 for at least writing your name on the booklet." "Ha-ha-ha."

I didn't know these guys then and don't know them now, but my bet is that they failed again that day.

Whenever I would participate in my 1L law school lectures (chats), discussion of the Baby Bar invariably surfaced. Most students seemed to be in awe of the extremely ominous 75 percent failure rate for first-time takers, almost as if they held the examination in reverence because it had slain so many of their fellow unaccredited brethren. As for me, all I could think of was being in the 25 percent that did pass on the first attempt. I never thought about going back a second time, and even looked forward to passing, at a minimum as a means of proving to myself that the correspondence method wasn't as big a joke as I thought it was. I can honestly remember taking my seat in the testing area that day, looking at the three people seated closest to me, and thinking, "Sorry, motherfuckers."

Again, when I took the CBX, I didn't know a single person that was there. This time, the venue was in my hometown, but still I didn't recognize a soul. Perfect.

My seat was at a two-person table that was at one end of a long row of approximately fifteen other such tables, or approximately thirty candidates. There was a guy seated next to me at the same table, and, of course, there was a table in front of us, in the next row, with two people seated there as well. I was already thinking that there were four of us sitting there in close proximity, and therefore, only me and one of the other three was going to make it, given the approximate 50 percent success rate for first-time takers.

Since I didn't want to talk to anyone about the examination, I never introduced myself to anyone, especially the guy sitting next to me, until the test was over on day three, and even then, it was brief at best. Although we had not spoken yet, I vividly remember noticing that he also kept to himself and showed up early like me. I figured he might be the other passer. Let's call him *"Quiet."*

The girl sitting directly in front of me was dressed fairly casually and was obviously from a local law school, since other candidates kept coming by and wishing her well. I really didn't know what to think about her at that point. Let's call her *"Local."*

After the initial reading of the examination instructions by the announcer-proctor had already begun, an older, disheveled man with thick glasses showed up. One of the proctors, roughly equivalent to him in age, approached and brought him an essay packet that was different in color from the rest of the essay packets that I could see. Based on their conversation, apparently he had initially registered as a laptop taker, but then changed his registration to handwriting taker at the last minute. As a result, he was going to be handwriting the examination among us laptop takers and was not in the handwriting section up front. Let's call him "*Toast.*"

When the announcer said "Go" to commence the morning session, I tore into the essay packet with ferocity, looking to conserve every possible second I could for outlining and writing. I didn't notice what *Local* did, but I did notice that both *Quiet* and *Toast* started off at a snail's pace. Literally, it seemed like they were afraid that the packet may contain anthrax or a bomb or some other nefarious contents that would harm them if they used any type of vigor whatsoever in opening it.

In practice, I typically outlined my essays in 10 minutes or less, which held true for the first essay I received that day. I was the first one of the four of us to begin writing (typing), followed by *Local*. *Toast* was still reading, but I figured he may have a different approach since he was wearing thick glasses and was handwriting the essay. I hadn't worn glasses since elementary school and hadn't handwritten anything since junior high school, so what the hell did I know anyway?

What surprised me was *Quiet*. I remember being at least 20 minutes into my essay before he ever hit a key on his laptop. When he did write something, it seemed like it was only a sentence or two, followed by a long pause. The silence was deafening.

In the afternoon session which was the PT, *Quiet* and *Local* were working feverishly, and so was I. PTs were not my strong suit, but even I knew that in order to get a decent grade on them you need to get the lead out of your ass. *Toast,* however, had seemed to have written just a few paragraphs, and then left the examination about a half hour early. He also took a couple of trips to the bathroom that seemed to last even longer than his scribing.

On day two, the MBE day, I felt like I was hung over without the antecedent benefit of having gotten drunk. Day one was so stressful and the parking lot was so congested with everyone trying to leave at the same time that when I finally made it home I was mental garbage. I remember dozing off early but waking up in the middle of the night and not being able to get back to sleep. In spite of being drained, I showed up early nonetheless, and *Quiet* and *Local* were punctual as well. *Toast*, however, almost didn't make it. He literally showed up about a minute before the announcer said "Go," earning him a reprimand from the proctor. In his absence, I can remember thinking that he probably had just quit after the previous day's piss-poor performance. He should have.

Day three was very similar to day one in terms of the conduct of my candidate neighbors, in spite of the fact that the morning session essays seemed to be much more of the racehorse variety than on day one, requiring even more speed. After the afternoon session PT was over, the CBX itself was finally over. I went ahead and decided to introduce myself to *Quiet* just to be polite. One of the first things out of his mouth was "I know I'll be back again."

"It wasn't as hard as I thought it would be, but my wife just had a baby and I haven't had time to study. I'm not even from here … I have to get to the airport to catch my flight home," he decried. It was almost as if this was scripted or rehearsed, because he even had a picture of his newborn as his laptop wallpaper.

On day one, when he didn't type very much and *Toast* didn't write very much, I knew that they were the two that would fail from our "group" of four. Our subsequent exchange of pleasantries paired with his quick defeatist statement, rationalized by personal issues, was merely a confirmation of this.

Candidates that fail the Bar Examination actually fail well before the announcer says, "Go." They fail when they look at the size of the examination and or the horrific statistics and begin to rationalize failure via the making of excuses. They fail when they go into the examination expecting to be one of the failing statistics because they had money problems, or work problems, or family problems, or relationship problems, or …

Under any type of objective analysis, a 50 percent first-time taker pass rate is discouraging. However, you can't just stop there and imagine how tough the examination must be, or how fortuitous the

50 percent that passed must be. Rather, you need to look beyond the mere numbers to the type of candidates that comprise the half that pass and the half that fail. You also need to take an introspective look at yourself.

Quiet should have never gotten on the airplane in the first place, since he failed back in his home state when he started cultivating excuses that sounded legitimate or worthy of sympathy. Sure, family is important, and I don't want to sound too callous, but if he really didn't have time to prepare, why was he even there—for the fun of it?

Toast should have stayed in bed, because if you can't show up punctually to one of the most important events of your life, you are failure incarnate, mate! Or alternatively, maybe he didn't think that the Bar Examination was one of the most important events of his life. Either way, it really doesn't matter when you take multiple trips to the bathroom during the test, each lasting about 10 minutes. Next time, *Toast*, take 11 minutes, and use that extra minute to kiss your ass good-bye while you are in there.

I already told you that I didn't know *Local* then, and don't know her now, but she was there punctually, wrote her ass off, and seemed to have a resilient bladder. I'm guessing *Local* passed.

Since I didn't talk to anyone except for that brief, emotional encounter with *Quiet*, the aforementioned is merely a recapitulation of my perception of these candidates during those 3 days in February. When the results came out in mid-May, perception surely became reality, harsh reality, for *Quiet* and *Toast*.

You see, I didn't talk to anyone, not just because I didn't know them or because I was being an antisocial ass, but instead, because I didn't want to get opinions from potential failing candidates about issue spotting, grading, or anything else to do with anything. I had done the math, looked at the statistics, and knew that one of every two candidates in there was going to fail—*excluding me*.

Why would I care what any other candidate in there opined about the examination? I had already worked my ass off to ensure that I knew more than they did! Why would I want to speak to people who speak loudly about failing in the past and getting the worst-possible score that anyone could get on an essay as long as they showed up and wrote something? A monkey with a keyboard could muster up a 40. For that matter, you could write a haiku on there and still get a 40!

Intimidation
Statistics so appalling
Excuse on standby

What ultimately matters with the Baby Bar and Bar Examination statistics is how you perceive, or interpret, them, and how this interpretation manifests itself in your preparation. You need to face the fact that there will be candidates that simply will not make it, but that you will not be one of them.

You will not be the candidate that is slow, late, and has a swan song on tap to make them feel better about their failure, since you will be studying so hard that there will be no time to even make any such excuses. This is my perception of you, since anyone that takes the time and initiative to read this book is obviously already taking the examination very seriously, and doing everything they can to pass.

When you walk in there to take that examination, you can choose to hear the insecurity, to see the despondency, to smell the fear and feel the pressure.

Or, on the other hand, you can choose to taste the victory!

Audio Files

AS PART OF my enrollment package, my law school sent me a set of audio recordings, on CD Rom, of all of the important rules, their elements, and definitions. Although I received the entire 4 years of subject matter upfront, presumably so that they could save on shipping, I think I listened to the 1L discs for about 2 months and never even bothered listening to the rest. Part of the reason for this was that they sounded like they were recorded in a bathroom, and the other reason was that they were doing me absolutely no good.

I had read posts of students that would listen to this junk when they were taking a shower, or driving, or even as they slept for subliminal stimulation. When I showered, I couldn't hear anything anyway, and even worse, I couldn't get out of the shower to stop the CD if it started to skip. When I was driving in Southern California, I was already pissed-off at the traffic and couldn't pay attention to this guy's monotone voice for the life of me. When I was sleeping, I was asleep. If I can't even remember my good and salacious dreams, there is no way that I'm going to remember this junk.

Admittedly, I was doing a lot of driving and commuting at the time, and thus could see the value in listening to useful audio recordings while in the car. For this, I started searching the Internet for commercially prepared, useful audio recordings (lectures) with good feedback ratings so that I could listen to them whenever I was in the car (alone). Not just rule statements or other hot air, but recordings of actual lectures that fully developed the subjects and their topics. I found them, and I bought them. You should too.

All the subjects from law school, the Baby Bar, and the Bar Examination are available. Thompson West produces *Sum & Substance*, and Gilbert Law Summaries produces *Law School Legends*. Both are great and a worthwhile investment.

My favorites, in case you care, were the Torts lecture from

Professor Steven Finz (from the multistate book), and the Contracts lecture from Professor Douglas Whaley, both on *Sum & Substance*. Professor Michael Kaufman also gives a practical and whimsical Agency and Partnership lecture on *Law School Legends*.

Fleming's also offers a robust set of audio lectures, paired with subject outlines, checklists, and practice essay questions, known as *The Exam Solution*. I think I purchased every subject they offer throughout law school, and as such, Jeff Fleming ultimately became my de facto law professor. Naturally, as I studied for both the Baby Bar and CBX, I continued to listen to the Fleming's audio lectures nonstop. While law study is fatally boring, Fleming does an incredible job of mixing humor and sarcasm with his lectures, thus, making the listening experience about as enjoyable as a law lecture can be. Fleming likes his job … and it shows.

When you listen to a lecture over and over again, regardless of its source, you start to remember it just like you would a song or movie. Once you remember it, you remember the definitions and or elements and also can easily skip to the parts where you are fuzzy or uncomfortable in the law. For example, if you have a problem with Defamation, keep listening to that topic until you have the lecture memorized. Conversely, skip past the Battery lecture if you already feel comfortable about harmful or offensive touching.

I've heard of some candidates actually going through hypnosis to help themselves calm down or better perform under the pressures of the examination. For me, memorizing so many parts of so many lectures was very calming, since if I would get stuck on the law somewhere during an examination, I would just think back to that long traffic jam on the 5 North.

On a quick, related note, during the CBX, I would return to my car during the lunch break, given the fact that my lunch would consist of merely a large cup of coffee and some random, light carbohydrate source. I had acquiesced to the parking rape perpetrated by the testing venue so that I could park underground where there was the closest proximity to the testing area. As far as I saw it, a few (lot) more bucks per day were worth some extra comfort and convenience at this stage of the game.

When I would return to my car and finish my coffee, I would notice other candidates in their cars as well, reading. By the looks (grimaces) on their faces, they were not reading an interesting novel or gossip rag, but rather, their notes and outlines. I never did this myself, since I figured that if I didn't know what I was doing by then, I was history anyway.

For me, the best use of this time was again the audio route. No, not more lectures, but rather music, good music, that would inspire me and get me in a good place. I would listen, think about how bad I wanted to pass this examination, and then listen some more. When I would go back in to the testing area after lunch, I was relaxed yet energetic, loose yet focused.

Those same candidates whom I saw reading probably saw me sitting there zoning out and thought I was crazy. Crazy is wasting that precious, nontest time to stress yourself out even more.

> "To see and listen to the wicked is already the beginning of wickedness."
> —*Confucius*

Exercism

EXERCISE HAS ABOUT as much to do with this book as do ski poles, so in passing, I want to make a brief mention of the fact that you need to make a point of getting some exercise while entrenched in your Baby Bar or Bar Examination review regimen.

Once you start studying, especially if you are hard-core about it like I was, you begin to feel like there is no time to do anything but study. This feeling can quickly turn into hysteria, preventing you from shaving, leaving the house, or doing anything other than studying, especially if you don't work, or work from home. Focus and dedication are good; cabin fever is not.

When I began studying, I quickly fell in to this trap of not getting outside enough and of seriously curtailing my exercising in favor of Draconian studying tactics. While prior to this I was no triathlete or anything of the sort, I was an avid mountain biker and generally made time for regular exercise. When I started to cut back, and then ultimately stopped riding and doing any exercising, my studying actually got worse, not better.

While the extra hour or so per day would, theoretically, give me more work or study time, the benefit of the extra time was nil as I began to feel more stressed out, less energetic, and less confident in my appearance. Staying away from exercising, particularly riding, also meant that I was ostracizing myself from my friends and the outdoors, which, in turn, made the study time seem that much less palatable.

When you exercise, particularly if you exercise hard, there is no time to think (worry) about studying, as all of your focus is trained on getting through the exercise task at hand. This is excellent, as both your body and mind are freed of the Baby Bar or Bar Examination study stress that can ultimately hold you back.

To reach a compromise with myself, I began to take my dog, or should I say he began to take me, for two longer walks per day. Not too long of walks, but long enough so that I could get outside, get away from studying, and get some kind of fresh air and exercise. I needed to walk him anyway, so this was a great way to kill two birds with one stone and not take up too much study time. When I walked him, I would listen to music, the same kind of music I would listen to during the CBX lunch breaks.

Since mountain biking can be a multiple-hour experience, and you can get pretty banged up if you are not careful, I wanted to avoid both a ride that was too lengthy, since I didn't want to get too worn out, as well as avoid a ride that would cause me to take the test in a cast, if at all. Instead, I began to go out riding maybe once or twice a week and for no more than an hour at a time. When I didn't do this, I would do some moderate working out at home for no more than 45 minutes or so. So, I was getting some cardio, either from walking my dog or riding, as well as some moderate-strength work on a daily basis.

If you never exercised before you started studying for the Baby Bar or Bar Examination, now would be a good time to start. Nothing major—no bodybuilding or marathon running—but merely something that will get your blood flowing and your mind off of the test. This will reduce stress and allow you to study more effectively, while concurrently building self-confidence.

Confidence begets confidence.

The May Tricks

AS WE HAVE already seen, the essay questions on the CBX are the largest-single source of points, and this is likely true for other Bar Examinations as well. Given this fact, any modicum of advantage that you can attain as it relates to the essays is of paramount importance to getting a passing total score.

Essay predictions are generally espoused by the Bar review companies, many times only a week or so before the examination. Other candidates are usually much quicker to offer up their unofficial predictions, or baseless guesses, on the forums and message boards of the law student websites. However, given the fact that any moron candidate can make an uneducated guess, and even worse, the fact that some candidates offer up bogus information just to screw with their competition, you'd probably be better off just going in there with no idea than to give credence to any of the unofficial, posted stuff. I simply made my own predictions.

Since the Baby Bar tests on only the same three subjects every time, you know going in to the examination that you will be writing at least one essay on Contracts, one on Criminal Law, and one on Torts. What you don't know is which one of the subjects will be tested twice. While predictions on such a limited subject base may appear to be unproductive, especially relative to the wide berth of the Bar Examination, the fact is that for a 1L, the Baby Bar feels like the Bar Examination, if not harder. On either examination, any beforehand idea of what subjects you are going to need to write on allows for more focused preparation and, hopefully, greater confidence.

Of the three subjects on the Baby Bar, the one that I disliked the most was Contracts. I always thought Criminal Law and Torts were more interesting, and therefore, studying them or writing essays about them always seemed a little bit easier. As such, I was hoping for only one Contracts essay on the Baby Bar, with the other three essays being a combination of one Criminal Law and two Torts, or one Torts and two Criminal Law, respectively. Since I really wanted to pass this thing, hoping alone wasn't good enough for me.

While each jurisdiction may vary, Calbar actually posts previous Baby Bar and CBX essay questions on their website, generally going back as far as 9 years. With two examination administrations per year, there are a total of up to eighteen past examination administrations, all in descending, chronological order. In order to make my own prediction based upon this data, I created a simple matrix within a spreadsheet, comprised of three rows labeled "Contracts," "Criminal Law," and "Torts." I then added columns labeled with each test administration date that was provided on the Calbar website.

Of the four essays on each examination administration, I would simply mark the corresponding box in my matrix with an uppercase "X" if that subject came up only once during that particular examination administration, and would mark the box with a double uppercase "XX" if the subject came up twice on the same examination administration. Since crossover essays, or essays of more than one subject, are also possible on the Baby Bar (and common on the CBX), I would mark the box with an uppercase and lowercase "Xx" if the subject was tested once alone and once as part of a crossover on the same examination administration. Here is a truncated example of what my matrix looked like when completed:

My Baby Bar Next June ⟶

	Jun	Oct	Jun	Oct	Jun	Oct	Jun	Oct
Contracts	X	XX	X	Xx	XX	X	X	XX
Criminal Law	X	X	XX	X	X	X	XX	X
Torts	XX	X	X	XX	X	XX	X	X

⟵

Based on this example and looking backward from right to left, I would take note that on the past three Baby Bar examination administrations, Contracts had been tested only once on two administrations, but then doubled up in the very last administration prior to the one I would be taking the following June.

Criminal Law had only been doubled up twice in the past eight administrations, and Torts was last doubled up three administrations prior. My prediction based on this information would then be a doubling up of Torts, since Contracts was just doubled up on the prior administration, and Criminal Law appeared to be rarely doubled up at all. While this is not scientific in the slightest, and furthermore, there is no guarantee that the Bar Examiners won't just throw darts at a dart board to determine the next examination lineup, to me, there was some discernable pattern. I was right.

Making this prediction early on did not mean that I ever neglected my studying of Contracts or Criminal Law in favor of Torts, because with only three subjects in total, there is no margin for error. However, at a minimum, the prediction gave me some added confidence that I would get a favorable series of essay questions, and, were I to screw up on the Contracts essay, I would have an extra Torts essay to make up some points.

I did this same process over again when it became time to start studying for the CBX.

However, due to the greater number of subjects and propensity for crossovers on the CBX, I knew that the semblance of any real pattern would not be realistic. Therefore, I focused my attention on two specific kinds of subjects: those subjects that seemed to always be tested, and, likewise, those subjects which had recently been neglected. In order to determine what these subjects were, I had to make another, bigger matrix. I referred to the Calbar site again, as well as the Fleming's CBX review materials, which included a very comprehensive, subject-specific list of when that subject had last appeared on the CBX, either as an essay, PT, or both. Fleming's is money.

Here is another, shortened matrix example:

◄ BARRIOR

My CBX
Next February
→

Subject	Feb	Jul	Feb	Jul	Feb	Jul
Agency/Partnership		x			x	X
Civil Procedure		X		X		
Community Property		x	x		x	X
Constitutional Law		X	X		x	
Contracts	x		X	x	Xx	
Corporations	X		x			
Criminal Law		X	x			x
Criminal Procedure	x	x		X		x
Evidence	X		x			X
Professional Resp	X	x	X	x	x	X
Property		x	X		x	
Remedies	x			X	x	
Torts	X			X	x	X
Wills/Trusts		x		X	X	

←

In this matrix, the uppercase "X" represents a complete essay on the subject, the lowercase "x" represents a crossover or single call in a multiple-call essay, and the uppercase and lowercase "Xx" represent a complete essay on the subject plus a crossover or single call in a multiple-call essay.

Based on this matrix, which is again similar to what my actual one looked like, looking backward from right to left, my essay predictions would be:

1. Civil Procedure
2. Constitutional Law
3. Corporations
4. Criminal Law
5. Property
6. Wills/Trusts
- Professional Responsibility (Crossover)
- Remedies (Crossover)
- Agency/Partnership (Wildcard)
- Evidence (Wildcard)

Aside from just looking at the blanks, I mixed in some logic.

Civil Procedure: Had been tested very infrequently in the past few years and was skipped entirely on the past two examination administrations. Also, at the time, there were two new developments to watch out for. One development was the fact that the United States Supreme Court had recently ruled that the "Nerve Center" test would be the test determinative of corporate citizenship, whereas before, there was a jurisdictional split regarding the "Muscle" test. The other development was the fact that the Bar Examiners had announced a couple of years prior that California Civil Procedure statutes and California Evidence statutes would now be fair game on the CBX. However, only California Evidence, and not California Civil Procedure, had ever been tested.

Constitutional Law: Had only been tested as a crossover or single call in a multiple-call essay once in the past three examination administrations. Moreover, Constitutional Law seems to be an essay favorite for the CBX given its robust spread of possible topics.

Corporations: Had been tested very infrequently in the past few years and was skipped entirely on the past three examination administrations. Also, "Business Associations" was now encompassing both Corporations and Agency/Partnership, and the Bar Examiners had begun starting to test Agency/Partnership much more than Corporations.

Criminal Law: Had only been tested as a crossover or single call in a multiple-call essay twice in the past four examination administrations.

Property: Had been tested only as a crossover or single call in a multiple-call essay once in the past three examination administrations. Moreover, Property seems to be an essay favorite for the CBX since most candidates abhor it.

Wills/Trusts: Had been skipped on the last examination administration prior to the one I would be taking in favor of Community Property. Community Property had been tested on almost every administration, to some degree, in recent years, so a stand-alone Wills/Trusts essay seemed more likely.

Professional Responsibility: Always seems to be tested on the CBX, usually as a crossover or single call in a multiple-call essay.

Remedies: Had been tested only moderately in the past few years, and additionally, always seems to sneak in, at a minimum, as a crossover or single call in a multiple-call essay. Besides, any candidate that wants to pass any subject essay must elaborate on damages or equity, where applicable, in order to get the good points.

Agency/Partnership: Had just been tested, but since this was a rather new addition to the CBX, I was anticipating a sneak attack repeat.

Evidence: Had just been tested as a criminal fact pattern with a call requesting the newly required California statutes. These California statutes had claimed many victims, so I was anticipating a sneak attack repeat, maybe in a civil fact pattern.

Here are the actual essays I received:

Day One

Essay 1:	Wills and Succession
Essay 2:	Constitutional Law
Essay 3:	Real Property

As you can see, all of these subjects had been predicted by me, and I went to lunch that day feeling pretty good. I could now scratch them off my list and do some quick review prior to day three on the other predicted subjects which had not yet surfaced.

Day Three

Essay 4:	Torts
Essay 5:	Business Associations (Corporations)/Professional Responsibility
Essay 6:	Remedies (Contracts)/Evidence

So I missed Torts and Contracts, but everything else had been anticipated. I went to lunch that day again feeling pretty good, especially since I knew by the looks on their faces that most of the other candidates had themselves either predicted wrong, or had no predictions at all, and had gotten torched. If their essays were not up to snuff, my essays would look that much better to the grader.

In sum, my predictions were generally very accurate, and I had made them months before I ever sat down and opened the essay packet (with ferocity). If you can do the same, and more important, can use the information wisely, predictions can definitely provide you with some level of advantage. In my case, I made a concerted effort to put in the work on these predicted subjects, at times favoring them to the subjects that I had not predicted. However, I didn't make a fool's gamble with my future, and ultimately, I studied all of the subjects to a degree with which I felt that I could write on them effectively if they appeared. Only a moron and a resultant failing candidate will use the predictions as a shortcut, focusing most of their study to writing only the essays that they believe they are going to get on the exam. This is both myopic and a manifestation of candidate indolence.

On that note, an equally inane use of the predictions is to believe in them so much that you are blinded by them. As I just mentioned, around the time that I took the CBX, the California statutes for Civil Procedure and Evidence were recent additions to the examination syllabus. The administration of the CBX prior to the one I would be taking had just tested on Evidence with California statutes for the first time, and yet, Civil Procedure with California statutes had never been tested. Even setting aside the addition of the California statutes, according to my matrix as well as the predictions of several Bar review companies, Civil Procedure was long overdue and was coming down.

Regardless, and proving that there is no exact science to predicting, there was no Civil Procedure, California or otherwise, on that examination. Notwithstanding, prior to the publishing of the "model" answers by Calbar, the forums and message boards of the law student websites were replete with postings from other candidates that had just taken the CBX, all of whom claimed to know the correct answer to Essay Six. I can't tell you how many posts I read that tried to convince the other readers that the Remedies, Contracts, and Evidence crossover was a Civil Procedure with California statues, Contracts and Remedies crossover. DOH!

While this essay was a son-of-a-bitch for other reasons, specifically that it was the last essay of the last day, was a racehorse, was comprised of a three-way crossover, and generally involved a funky fact pattern, there was no Civil Procedure to be found, California statutes or otherwise. In fact, the first call of the question spoke to the admission of testimony (Evidence) and the second call spoke to the party's claims for relief. The claims for relief were Reformation and Rescission, respectively (Remedies), which could only be developed via an analysis of the contract (Contracts). So why did some candidates write on Civil Procedure with California statutes when it was nowhere to be found?

I can only guess that they wrote on Civil Procedure with California

THE MAY TRICKS

statutes because in recent months all of the Bar review companies had been predicting that either Civil Procedure or Evidence with California statutes were going to materialize, and when Evidence with California statutes came down on the prior examination administration, everyone was sure that the long overdue Civil Procedure would turn up on the subsequent CBX, and in the form of California statutes. When the candidates saw "Answer according to California law" on the call of the question, some were apparently so brainwashed by the Bar review predictions that they defied all logic.

I hope that they didn't make the same mistake again when they retook the examination.

Do yourself a favor and take the time to make your own matrix and your own predictions. Use the predictions as a guide for prioritizing and focusing your study efforts when needed, and also for ensuring that you can handle an essay question in one of the predicted subjects.

Don't do yourself a disfavor and merely rely upon someone else's predictions, and furthermore, don't fall into the laziness trap of studying only what you predict. Above all, don't rely upon any predictions, regardless of their genesis, to a fault (like the Civil Procedure candidates did). If the essay looks like a duck and quacks like a duck, it's a duck.

> Interviewer: "What's your prediction for the fight?"
> Clubber Lang: "My prediction?"
> Interviewer: "Yes, your prediction."
> Clubber Lang: "Pain."
>
> —*Rocky III* (1982)

Checkered Passed

AS FAR AS I'm concerned, subject checklists are the single most effective study aid for both the Baby Bar and Bar Examination, as well as law school, for that matter. Once I started using checklists in preparation for my impending Baby Bar, I never looked back. Checklists are not a new concept, or anything that I myself conceptualized, and, in fact, there may be some of you who are using them now. If you are unfamiliar with the checklist, it is akin to a course outline that must be completed or filled in, rather than merely read or reviewed. Think of a flash card that is blank on the back, so rather than reading the answer, you need to write it in.

Here is an example of what a checklist template may look like:

Sample Template — Contracts Checklist

Contract Formation
1. Offer
2. Acceptance
3. Consideration

And here is an example of what the corresponding checklist blank might look like:

Sample Blank — Contracts Checklist

Contract Formation
1.
2.
3.

As with the example immediately above, when you do a checklist, you are required to complete the blank based on your ability to recall the corresponding information, and when you are both recalling information and reinforcing that recall through writing, the reinforcement is what ultimately creates retention. The more you do them, the quicker the retention.

I first learned of the checklist when taking my Baby Bar review course with Fleming's. Fleming's included template and blank checklists which the candidates could copy and use, which was great, until I memorized everything within a week.

These prepared checklists were not that different from the example above. While they were effective to get me thinking about the big issues while I was outlining an essay or doing an MBE question, they simply did not have enough substance to help *me* master the exam. Then again, they weren't supposed to. You see, when you use prepared outlines, checklists, or even flash cards, you are buying a generic, one-size-fits-all study aid that is meant to be adequate for any cross section of students or candidates. If you obtain these materials from another student or candidate who made them for themselves, you are likewise getting a one-off that caters specifically to that person and not yourself.

When I started to do Fleming's checklists, I had what I would call a relative epiphany since I quickly realized that for me this was the best way to memorize the law and recall it at will. When I was able to memorize all these big-ticket items within a week, I knew that I could add more and more items to my own checklists and memorize it all within a few weeks.

This is where you separate the passers from the repeaters. It takes a lot of time and introspection to look at each specific subject and each specific topic of each subject and determine what you really need on your checklist and what you don't, not to mention the time it takes to make the template and the blank, and then the time to do them on a daily basis. Some of the bulkier subjects, like Constitutional Law or Property, could take several days to make, especially if there is a lot of material that you feel like you need to include in your checklist. Other

CHECKERED PASSED

subjects may take less time, either because they are not as robust, you feel more comfortable with the material already, or a combination thereof.

So how do you make a checklist for yourself?

First and foremost, you need to do this on a computer. A good checklist is always in a state of flux, and therefore, you need the ability to add, delete, or edit information at will. Moreover, each time you change the template, the blank will need to change accordingly as well. Also, if you are creating your checklist while you are still in law school or in preparation of the Baby Bar, you will want to save these so that you can dust them off again in preparation for the Bar Examination.

In the case of the preprepared Baby Bar checklists that I had received from Fleming's, all of the major topic areas of each subject were already delineated, so I merely used their topic areas as a starting point. I figured that since they had taken the time to condense and focus the review to its most salient subjects and topics, I would follow their lead. With a major topic area in place, I would begin by perusing their review outline to look more in-depth at the subjects and topics, determining what I specifically needed to know and memorize. Additionally, I would refer to the table of contents in one of my outline books from law school, like Emanuel or Gilbert, and would verify that my checklist covered all of the major subjects.

When done, my first draft was very long and very complete. Each checklist would encompass the entire subject, including the main topics, subtopics, rules, exceptions, rule splits, mnemonics, or whatever I felt was important for me to know (memorize).

How did I know what was important for me to know?

I did my first checklists in preparation for the Baby Bar after I had already completed the three subjects during my 1L studies. As with all students, there were some aspects of each subject that I just got, and others that I did not. If there was something that I just got, I might make a cursory mention of it on the checklist but go no further. If I had a hard time with a topic, I might list it, put the rule, and then add anything else I thought I needed.

When I started doing checklists for my 2L-4L studies in law school, since by now I was sold on the concept after what I was able to do in my Baby Bar studies, I would start the course off obviously not knowing anything. For me, the best way to learn was to make a checklist, using either Fleming's *The Exam Solution* for each subject, and or the table of contents from my law school outline books. Since I knew nothing of the subject yet, I would include everything that looked important and simply adjusted accordingly as the year went by. By adjusting accordingly, I mean that I would remove stuff that I just seemed to understand or figured that I knew really well, and conversely, might even add more stuff if that was what I needed.

As you can imagine, making the checklists for law school was a drawn-out process that required many edits. Once I had the checklist made and began using it, it was worth every minute I had invested. Within a couple of months of beginning a new course, I had cursory knowledge of everything. By the time I was scheduled to take my finals, I was not worried about getting tested on anything since I knew that I knew enough about all of it.

Theoretically, most of you are Bar Examination candidates or proximate candidates, and, thus, you have already completed, or significantly completed, the courses that will be on your forthcoming examination. You now know then what topics of each subject were (are) problematic for you, and what topics you have comfort with. Armed with this knowledge, you can create your own custom-tailored checklists for the Baby Bar or Bar Examination, dedicating more substance where needed and less where it is not.

If you are doing the amount of MBEs that you need to be doing, and writing the amount of essays that you need to be writing, what needs to be on your checklist will become more and more evident. There are just some things that get tested over and over again, and these are the things that you must know. In fact, by missing MBE questions and reading the explanation of the correct answer, I learned things that I had never learned in law school. I would usually add this stuff to my checklist.

Also, when I would read a sample Baby Bar or Bar Examination essay answer, either as provided to me by Fleming's or the Calbar website, I would make note of the things that I had never learned in law school and would add these to my checklist as well. Sometimes I would edit the checklist in the computer, or sometimes I would just scribe manual notes onto my template. No matter how I added it, it got added for one important reason: if this was a passing essay and it included that information, I too would need to include that information to pass.

After you create a checklist for each subject, what next?

If you have approximately fifteen subjects that will be tested on the Bar Examination, there is no way to do every checklist on a daily basis. Rather, you might start with a 5-day rotation, doing three subject checklists per day. As the Bar Examination draws closer, you may end up on a 3-day rotation doing five checklists per day. The Baby Bar, with only three subjects, permits daily checklist work of all three subjects.

For the reasons I stated above, I am not going to provide you with my own checklists in this book. Moreover, and even though it pains me to say this, I won't even sell them to you separately either, since that would ultimately be counterproductive to your success. What I will do is provide you with a partial sample of what one of mine looked like, and from there, you just need to get busy getting busy on creating your own, the sooner the better.

Sample Template—*Real Property Checklist*

Joint Interest in Real Property

> **Joint Tenancy:** Right of survivorship
> 1. CL: Presumed ML: Created by act of parties

2. Four unities
   (1). Possession: Right to use the whole property
   (2). Interest: Equal interest
   (3). Title: Must acquire interest by same instrument
   (4). Time: Interest must be acquired at the same time
3. Terminate unilaterally by: a) Partition suit b) Inter vivos conveyance
4. Mortgage: a) Lien theory (Maj) – No severance; surviving takes subject to mortgage
   b) Title theory (Min) – Severance
   c) 1 JT can't unilaterally mortgage more than his/her own share
5. Lease: CL: Severs ML: Contra

Tenancy in Common: Unity of possession
ML presumes: If conveyance
Terminate by: a) Partition b) Tenants join to sell

Sample Blank—Real Property Checklist

Joint Interest in Real Property

Joint Tenancy:
1. CL: ML:
2. Four unities
   (1).   :
   (2).   :
   (3). :
   (4). :
3. Terminate unilaterally by: a)   b)
4. Mortgage: a)   (Maj) –
   b)   (Min) –
   c)
5. Lease: CL: ML:

Tenancy in Common:
1. ML presumes:
2. Terminate by: a)   b)

If I give you fish, you will eat for a day. If I teach you to fish, you will tell your friends and they will buy my fishing poles.

¿Que Passit Essay?

WHEN YOU SEE the scores of those candidates that have previously failed the Baby Bar or Bar Examination, one thing that they all share in common is mediocre to poor essay scores. The fact is that no matter how well you know or think you know a subject, and no matter what grades you received in law school, there is nothing that can better prepare you to effectively write a Baby Bar or Bar Examination essay than to write these very essays in practice.

The first step in this process is to figure out a plan for writing an equivalent number of essays from each subject. For the Baby Bar, this means Contracts, Criminal Law, and Torts. For this task, I created yet another matrix within a spreadsheet, comprised of one row for each subject. Then I would place an uppercase "X" next to that subject whenever I wrote a complete essay on it, and a lowercase "x" whenever I wrote a crossover essay or answered a single call on the subject in a multiple-call question. This way, I could easily see at a glance how many essays I had written for each subject, and therefore, I would know which subject should be written about next. When all three subjects had the same number of "X" indicators listed, I would just start back from the top, doing one Contracts, one Criminal Law, and one Torts essay.

When it came time to study for the CBX, I utilized the same type of system, placing an uppercase "X" next to the subject when I wrote a complete essay on it and a lowercase "x" when I wrote a crossover essay or answered a single call on the subject in a multiple-call question.

Even with only three subjects, the Baby Bar required me to keep track of what I had written, primarily since I was so preoccupied with studying that I became absentminded in other areas, and simply did not want to make the mistake of not getting uniform essay work. With the CBX, there are so many subjects and so many essays to be written

◀ BARRIOR

that it is absolutely essential to keep a record of what you have done and what needs to be done.

Here is an example of what my matrix looked like for the CBX:

Corporations	X	X	X	X
Agency/Partnership	X	x	X	
Civil Procedure	X	X	X	X
Community Property	x	X	X	X
Constitutional Law	X	X	X	X
Contracts	X	X	X	
Criminal Law	X	x	X	x
Criminal Procedure	X	x	X	
Evidence	X	X	X	X
Professional Resp	X	x	x	
Property	X	X	X	X
Remedies	X	X	x	
Torts	X	X	X	X
Wills/Trusts	x	X	X	X

Using this example, had I planned to write only one essay today, I would choose from either Agency/Partnership, Contracts, Criminal Procedure, Professional Responsibility, or Remedies, as these five subjects had less "Xs" than the other subjects. Of these subjects, Professional Responsibility had only been a crossover or single call in a multiple-call question on the past two essays I had written, and therefore, as a subject, it had received the least amount of essay writing of the five aforementioned subjects. However, if I felt pretty good about Professional Responsibility, I might write on one of the other foregoing subjects instead if I felt that I really needed more work in that particular subject. When there is a toss-up or when in doubt, always write more essays on the subjects where you know you are weakest.

As I have previously mentioned, I had hundreds of former Baby Bar and CBX essays, provided to me both by Fleming's, as well as those published on the Calbar website. With a plethora of essays and a system for keeping track of my writing, it was time to get writing.

I would always start by clearing off my desk, leaving only those essays which I was going to write and some blank scratch paper. I would keep the essays turned over or covered until I was ready to begin, and I would close my door, shut off my phone, and close my email so that I would not be distracted. As the examination date drew nearer, I would remove the external keyboard from my laptop since during the examination I was not going to use one. Likewise, I would begin writing the essays directly into the laptop testing software program that I had downloaded in order to be permitted to use the laptop on the examination. This can be done in a "practice test" environment, and again, I did this since this was the program that I was going to have to use during the actual examination, and I wanted to be familiar with it.

Of course, creating Bar-like conditions would otherwise be pointless without limiting my essay time to one hour per each essay to be written. If I was writing one essay, I would stop at a maximum of one hour, and generally would try to write for the entire time. This means that if I finished an essay in 55 minutes, I wouldn't stop early, but rather would use the last 5 minutes to add more, be it facts, argument, bolding, underlining, or do anything extra that I could do to help my score. If I was writing two essays, I would stop in 2 hours, meaning that maybe I would spend 55 minutes on one essay and 65 minutes on the other essay. Knowing how much time to allot to each essay was a skill that I developed over time, a skill which never would have developed had I not written countless essays under timed conditions.

In fact, of those candidates that do poorly on the essays, many complain of running out of time or spending too much time on one exam and thereby being forced to sacrifice the next exam. In actuality, most likely, it is not that these candidates didn't know the law or didn't study the rules hard enough, but instead, they didn't write enough essays under timed conditions and, thus, never learned how to quickly determine where to allocate the minutes. Constant practice is the only way to learn this.

When I would begin the essay, the first thing that I would do is write the time down on the top right-hand corner of my scratch paper, which would subsequently become my outline. I did this same thing during the Baby Bar and CBX as well, since the only way to effectively manage your time is to know how much of it you have left. During the heat of battle, it is easy to forget the exact hour and minute, and there is simply no margin for error. After I wrote down the time, I would put my pencil or pen down and start by reading the call of the question. By the way, I preferred to use a pencil so that I could erase rather than scratch out information if necessary. When your outline is cluttered, it just makes it that much harder to effectively and efficiently read.

After I read the call of the question, I would then read the fact pattern (still without a writing implement in my hand). The first read is a read only, not a read and write.

After reading the fact pattern once, I would read the call of the question again, and then, depending on the length of what I had read, or my level of confusion at the time, I might read all or part of the fact pattern one more time. I never wanted to start creating the outline unless I felt like I completely understood what was being asked of me. Don't jump the gun to save a minute or two because in the end, any mistakes you make will cost you double that time.

Now, with pencil in hand, I would start creating a brief outline, listing the issue, then relevant exceptions, splits, or crucial facts such as an important date in Wills/Trusts. Outlining is a task which must be done on every essay, as you need to have a place to create your essay's infrastructure. I always kept mine contained on one side of a single sheet of paper, and likewise, never put down the rule statement, or any facts either, unless they were of utmost import. Also, depending on the fact pattern, I might write down something like "Liable" or "Not Guilty."

Here is an example of what an outline of mine might look like for a Negligence issue:

<u>Negligence</u>
Special Duty–Minor?
Prox. Cause–Intervening Act?
Loss of Consortium

<u>*Liable*</u>

As you can see, there are a lot of things that never made it on the outline, like most of the elements, rule statements, and specific facts. Since I had been doing my checklists religiously, I knew the elements and rule statements cold and only needed to make these brief points to remind me to bring them up. If there were no facts that were so important as to occupy space on my outline, they didn't. Rather, I would just underline them or circle them on the test itself or write something on the outline like "Paragraph 2" so that I could pull them directly from the examination. When I would write, I would always have my outline and my essay question side-by-side or one above the other, always continuously referring to both throughout my writing. Some candidates use book stands for this, but I always found it easier just to lay them flat on the table. By the way, a typical reading and then outlining should take approximately 10 minutes, but no more than 15. When you get good, this drops to 7 to 10 minutes maximum.

Once you have your outline crafted and are ready to begin writing, the time factor will come in to play. Time will dictate how much discussion can be dedicated to each issue, or even whether an issue should be left out of the essay due to a lack of time. Sometimes you may create an outline that contains some issues which are the principal issues, and additionally, you may include collateral issues that may also be plausible to argue. Oftentimes, the collateral issues are gems that generate good points on your essay since most of the other candidates missed them or simply did not have time to write about them.

On my CBX, Essay Four, on day three, was a racehorse Torts exam. As soon as I read the multiple calls of the question I knew this, as there were multiple parties and multiple issues. Since I had written so many essays in practice, I figured that this might be a sixty–sixty-two minute exam, and I also knew that the graders would be looking for all of the subissues that were included. As with most racehorse exams, the main issues were pretty easy to spot, so the difference between a good score and a poor score lies in spotting the subissues.

Because this was a racehorse, most candidates probably struggled just to get the main items on the paper within an hour. I knew that I could hammer this stuff out, and I also knew that I had to add these extra goodies to differentiate my essay. My practice gave me the confidence to take a couple of extra minutes, if need be, because I knew I could make it up on the next essay.

This was a Torts essay, not an Agency essay, but the Vicarious Liability–*Respondeat Superior* issue begged for a one-sentence analysis of the assent, benefit, and control between agent and principal. This one sentence would be something that most other candidates would never think of including, and thus, the reader would perceive my essay to be more complete. Now, if I were short on time, I could have easily left this out too, just making mention of *Respondeat Superior*. The reality is that oftentimes there are issues on your outline that you simply don't write about in the essay, either because you know from your experience that you don't have the time, or you realize once you start writing that they are really too tangential to be of any point value, and, thus, a waste of time.

By contrast, Essay Two on day one was a Constitutional Law essay that specifically asked about the merits of a challenge based upon the Free Exercise Clause and the Establishment Clause of the First Amendment, respectively. This was not a racehorse and the two major issues were provided in the call of the question. Since I knew that the points here would be derived from arguing the facts to the rules of both the Free Exercise Clause and Establishment Clause, my outline was pretty bare since I knew the rules in my head and the facts were all on the examination itself. I also knew that I could outline and write this essay well in 50–55 minutes, and that without many issues, the argument, or application of facts to the issues, would be the whole enchilada.

No matter how proficient I became at outlining, invariably, I would begin writing and then stumble across a new issue that I had not originally seen and therefore had not put on my outline. This is a good problem to have if you have the time and the skill to make adaptations on the fly, since, instead of missing a more obscure issue, you have uncovered it and will get points for it. However, if you don't practice your essay writing enough, you will never see these issues in the first place, which is also, relatively, probably a good problem, since you would never have the time or the skill to make adaptations on the fly anyway.

When you do start writing the essay, be sure to write like a lawyer since you are writing to a lawyer who simply happens to be grading your essay. When there is a landmark case like _Miranda v. Arizona_ (no relation), make sure you spell it correctly. Also, while the Bar Examiners claim that grammar and spelling are not considered in your grade, you know that an essay with a significant number of misspellings and grammatical flaws will not look lawyerlike, and thus, will ultimately negatively influence the grader's decision. As far as influencing positively is concerned, always use the most erudite lexicon as possible. Instead of putting a headnote on a Contracts essay that reads, "Common Law or UCC?" try putting "Governance," and then distinguish between the common law and the UCC in your writing. If you have a headnote related to the Tenth Amendment in Constitutional Law, don't put "10th Amendment" but rather spell out "Tenth Amendment." Even better, spell out "Federalism–Tenth Amendment." "In the case at bar" just sounds smarter than "Here," just as "arguendo" sounds smarter than "for the sake of argument."

You are done with your essay when you hit the time limit, whether or not you finished. If you keep typing after they call time during the examination, you will get reported to the Bar Examiners. While practicing, if you keep writing after the time is up, you are only practicing ineffectuality.

After you are finished writing, proceed to review your work product against a sample or "model" answer. This is the only way to see where you are strong and where you are weak, but you also need to be careful about giving too much credence to the model answer.

Some Bar review courses, like Fleming's, will provide you with an actual Baby Bar or Bar Examination essay and the corresponding answer that the candidate wrote, including the grade that they received. These are good because they give you an idea of what that kind of score looks like. However, these can also be bad because they were written by another candidate who may not have fully developed the essay. A model answer by contrast is generally a very complete essay that covers just about everything. However, it was written under nontimed conditions with the aid of an open book, and anyone could write such an answer under those circumstances.

The best way to review your essays, then, is to put everything in context. If the sample Baby Bar or Bar Examination answer got a good score, look to see what they have on their answer that you missed, and also look for things that you simply didn't know, like rule splits or exceptions, and then add these things to your checklist so that you never miss them again. If the sample Baby Bar or Bar Examination answer has a bad score, don't try to take too much from it other than using it as a gauge of your own work and potential score.

On the model answers, just don't feel too bad if yours is not nearly as good, since, again, writing under non-Bar conditions is not the point. Either way, look again for law or rule splits that you may not already know, and also look to see if they saw all the issues that you saw. I can't tell you how many model answers I read that omitted some issues or subissues that my answer actually did contain.

As you go through this process, keep track of the essays that gave you a lot of trouble and make some sort of indication on them that will permit you to return and redo them, or at least review them, before the examination. After I would write an essay, I would put it in a folder with all of the other essays of that subject that I had written. If the particular essay gave me problems, I would color the top right-hand corner with a highlighter.

I knew that the chance of being tested on a similar fact pattern on my Baby Bar and CBX was real, since the more essays you write the more you realize that the same general issues and fact patterns tend to reemerge. Rather than just hope that it didn't happen, I had to prepare.

By the time the Baby Bar arrived, I had a handful of essays that I had flubbed during practice. The last essays that I wrote while studying for the Baby Bar, therefore, were these essays, since I needed to get confident that I could handle them if I saw something similar on examination day.

When the CBX arrived, I had several essays, primarily in Property, that were colored on the top right-hand corner. I had decided that the Sunday and Monday before the examination I would go through all of these, as well as all the other ones from other subjects that were colored, in an effort to get a better understanding of what I did wrong since the same type of essay could surface on Tuesday or Thursday.

Now, I do not usually believe in merely outlining an essay or reading an essay and then reviewing the model answer as opposed to writing an essay. This is what the lazy candidate does who then complains that they ran out of time and got a 55 or worse. Except as discussed below, always outline the essays, and then write them out completely under timed conditions.

With only a couple of days left and a seeming rainbow of colored essays to review, I simply did not have the time to rewrite all of the essays at this late stage. Rather, I outlined them to make sure that I could spot the right issues, and then read the answers to make sure that the outline was right. At this point, I had my timing down cold, so if there was ever a moment to just outline and review that would not affect my overall performance, this was it.

One of the major problems I had had with Property was Covenants Running with the Land, Equitable Servitudes, and Implied Reciprocal Easements. Easements were good, landlord-tenant was cool, but the running problems always seemed to screw me up. Since I had been predicting that Property was going to be one of my essays, I knew that I had to be ready for this just in case. After outlining the exams that had previously given me trouble, then reading the answers again and again if necessary, I felt like I had enough in the brain pan to handle one if it showed up. It showed up. Essay Three on day one was a Property exam, and it was primarily Covenants Running with the Land and Equitable Servitudes. A week ago, this was my worst nightmare; today, it was a wet dream.

Being a lawyer requires a lot of writing, even if you are a litigator or even if you have a law clerk or paralegal that you can delegate most of your tasks to. This is why the Bar Examiners allocate the largest percentage of points to writing, and this is why you need to allocate the largest percentage of your Baby Bar or Bar Examination study to writing.

> "There is nothing to writing. All you do is sit down at a typewriter and bleed."
>
> —*Ernest Hemingway*

PT Loser

IF YOU ARE taking the Baby Bar, you have dodged a bullet, for now, but if you are taking the CBX, you are going to be shot with two, three-hour PTs. Other Bar Examinations will likely serve up two of the more manageable one-and-a-half hour Multistate Performance Tests ("MPTs"). If you have never done a test of either variety, watch out.

I personally despised the PT, due, in large part, to the erroneous yet well-intentioned advice that was given to me by my lawyer friends, all of whom I had met during my internship. Essentially, they each told me that they only did five or six PTs before they took the CBX, since there was really nothing that could be studied for anyway. All of them also told me that I should have no problem with it since I was adept at writing motions. Only one of them had actually passed the CBX on the first attempt.

Just the specter of having to do one single test for 3 hours, then spending at least another half an hour reviewing the answer, made me cringe, so I put off the PTs as long as I could, in lieu of doing MBEs and writing essays. In retrospect, this was a big mistake, and likewise, was the reason why the PT was surely my lowest-scoring component on the CBX.

Putting off, and ultimately waiting too long, to begin working the PTs meant that I first opened Fleming's lectures and review materials on this component with only about 7 weeks remaining before the CBX. Maybe if I were a speed-reader or a candidate that had actually learned the skill of case briefing in law school this would have been sufficient, but I wasn't, and it wasn't.

Before I get any further into this, I want to point out that the Fleming's method for doing PTs is, well, the Fleming's method for doing PTs. With that being said, if you want to know the specifics, you are going to need to take their course or purchase their materials. Even if I wanted to share it with you, I couldn't do it justice anyway.

Like I just said, this was surely my lowest-scoring component on the CBX.

The review course that I received was taught by attorney Susan Sneidmiller, who has apparently done every PT since their introduction to the CBX in 1984. Sneidmiller clearly understands every aspect of this test, and it shows, given the girth of the review book and the ample discussion in the lectures. She also has a quick wit and cynical nature like Fleming, which makes the otherwise dreadful course bearable.

However, because of its comprehensive nature, in retrospect, I would have rather taken the review course live as opposed to home study. This would have permitted me the opportunity to not only ask questions, but also get a better sense of what the other candidates were doing and not doing with the material. While I usually did not care what other candidates did since I felt that I did it better, I did believe that there was a broader, user-specific interpretation of the method that could be employed, yet I simply did not have the right perspective in my ostracism of home study.

So, as a nonspeed-reader, when I did attempt to read through these tests at a very quick pace, I would have a tendency to miss important facts and or fail to glean the big picture. As a result, I would spin my wheels for several minutes and still be stuck in park. Right away, I would feel stupid and also would doubt my ability to finish the test successfully.

Being that I was a deplorable case briefer only added salt to the wound. Sure, I had some cases to brief for each course I took in law school, but not enough of them to really develop any noteworthy briefing skills. Moreover, most of the cases were of the landmark variety, so I already knew from my lectures or my outlines what they were all about. Regurgitating this was not really a problem, nor was it truly briefing. While you don't need to do an actual case brief to work a PT, you do need to understand the fundamentals of briefing, and likewise, need to be comfortable with the confusing terminology. If you are not so comfortable, depending on the amount of time remaining before your examination, get comfortable.

As if confusing cases weren't enough, the Library also oftentimes contains codes, factors, judicial tests, or other refuse which you will be forced to decipher. My best advice to you here is to read the separators carefully, to wit "or" or "and." Obviously, if you have an "or," you only need to satisfy one requirement, and if you have an "and," you need to satisfy more than one requirement. I screwed this up a lot when reading too fast, and it killed me.

The real deal breaker in all of this was ultimately my penmanship—I can't handwrite legibly to save my life. The honest and embarrassing fact is that after I took a typing course in high school I never really handwrote any of my assignments anymore, preferring to type everything on the computer. As I got older and did all of my work on the computer, emailed instead of writing letters by hand, and so forth, my handwriting skills atrophied to the point of illegibility.

Cover your ears, but when you are creating an outline by which to write a PT, and then realize when you go to write the PT that you can't even read your own handwriting, bluntly stated, you are fucked.

Exacerbating all of these problems was the fact that I would wait until the end of the day after I had finished my other Bar Examination study to do the PT. Suffice it to say that the evening after a long day of study is not the best time to try and write a PT, but I was intentionally procrastinating. When I would mess the PT up, I would get frustrated and then would have trouble sleeping, which, in turn, began to mess with everything else that I was doing. I actually called one of my lawyer friends at 11:00 p.m. one night in a panic, having just come unglued after trying, unsuccessfully, to get through a PT earlier that evening. He told me that he wouldn't have taken my call except that he thought it must be an emergency since I would usually only text him, and never this late.

It was an emergency in my eyes. To his credit, he spent a good 30 minutes or so trying to sort out the finer points of PT strategy with me, from what he could remember anyway, from when he took the CBX. He even offered to sit down with me and go over a couple of tests if I wanted to.

Another lawyer friend of mine, Attorney, actually, did sit down with me to go over this stuff. He took one look at my outline and said, "That's not you. That's not how you write." He was right, yet the only real advice he could give me at that point was to treat these PTs like the motions I had written for him.

While fundamentally this was sound advice, the motions I had written for him were usually never done in 3 hours' time, unless, of course, they were very brief motions. As such, when I got home from his office that afternoon, I began to scour the Internet looking for any tips or tricks I could find, ideally from other candidates that had grappled with the same issues as me. Tips or tricks that would, notwithstanding my particular defects, permit me to assemble the building blocks and put forth an adequate answer within the allotted time.

I saw that there were a couple of other instructors out there that claimed that they had the silver bullet for slaying the PT, but the CBX was fast approaching and I had no time to go through another course. Moreover, I didn't want to spend more money on somebody else's course just to come back to the same realization that the problem was not the method, it was me.

What I did read somewhere was that the MPTs were fundamentally the same as the PTs, except, of course, that the MPT is only half as long. Since this meant that that if I wrote an MPT, it would take half as much time out of my day, so I figured that this would be a good place to cut my teeth and start to make some tweaks. Another good thing about the MPTs is that on the NCBE website, you can get up to twenty of the former examinations for free, including the Point Sheets used for grading them.

The first time I did an MPT I realized that just having half as much to comb through made a world of difference, as it just looked more manageable. This alone reduced the stress significantly.

When I would read through the Point Sheets to check my answer when I was done, as opposed to reading some superhuman candidate's answer or some model answer that was crafted over the course of a week and not in 3 hours, I better realized that there existed a good deal of flexibility and subjectivity in the answer as long as the major points were addressed.

Since these MPTs were to be my new, manageable proving ground, I began to explore different ways of reading the content and then making an outline, different ways that were more conducive to my way of conceptualizing and writing.

I would begin by breaking down the call of the question on the assignment Memorandum and listing each part on the top of what would ultimately become my outline. Since many times a one-paragraph call can contain multiple assignments, I wanted to be sure that this was crystal clear to me before I ever started anything. Also, if the Memorandum told me not to do something, I would highlight this and or circle it.

There were many times when I first started doing the PTs that I missed assignments that I was tasked with completing, and, likewise, while I am embarrassed to admit this, I once even created a Table of Contents, having not fully read the Memorandum which told me not to do it. Think about taking the Bar Examination and wasting 20 minutes making a Table of Contents that no other candidate likely made. You would not only run out of time, but your answer would also stand out, in an übernegative sense, to the grader who had the misfortune of receiving it. 40.

Once I had a handle on what I needed to do and refrain from doing, I figured that reading of any of the contents, be it the File or the Library, was useless if I didn't ultimately understand what I had just read. I decided then that I would read the File once, completely, and at a moderate speed, and highlight the things that I thought might be of value, including various facts like dates, monies, and other tidbits that seemed like they were put there for a reason. Next, I would read the Library once, completely, and at a moderate speed, highlighting the codes that seemed relevant to the File I just read, as well as highlighting or circling the main issues and the most succinct rules of those issues. If there were any factors, judicial tests, interesting *dicta*, or a sound case holding, I would mark all of that too, usually in a different color highlighter to help distinguish it from the issues and rules.

Also, I always made a point of looking for footnotes, since usually there was something of value contained within the miniscule, veiled text. Again, when I first started working the PTs, I missed a lot of stuff by failing to ever read the footnotes.

Now that I felt that I understood a bit better what I had just read in both the File and the Library, I would begin to make a rudimentary outline and try to piece it all together. Sometimes the assignment Memorandum would tell me what the issues were and what I needed to do, and sometimes I just needed to figure out the issues and then do what I needed to do. Either way, I would start just like I was creating an outline for an essay. Following the IRAC, or Issue, Rule, Application, and Conclusion approach, I would go back to what I had highlighted or circled in the Library and pick the main issues, either from the codes, the cases, or both, and would use that as my starting point. The issue is whatever the codes or cases are addressing.

If there were codes, I would just put the code number down on the outline under the respective issue I had listed rather than write it out. Proceeding then to the cases, I would find the most salient rule, or multiple rules if more than one case dealt with the very same issue, and would write down on my outline an abbreviated case name and the page number where the rule was, as well as a very truncated explanation of what the rule stated. Again, I put this under the respective issue I had listed. I would also put a check mark on that page next to the rule(s) in the Library so that I could ferret out the precise verbiage more easily when I went back to write. When there were two cases that dealt with the same issue, usually one case had a rule that was beneficial to my position and the other was a rule that was not so beneficial. I would write a "+" or "-" next to the case name just so that I could distinguish this when I started to write.

When I had this outline seemingly ready at this juncture with the issues and rules, I would then go back to the File and look for the facts that would be the basis of the application in the IRAC. I might jot these down in an abbreviated fashion on my outline next to the rules if I could, or maybe would just list a page number if there were a cluster of facts or figures in one spot within the File. Again, I did not always copy the facts into the outline, and if I did, it was extremely brief, at best.

When I started writing, I would always take another look at the Memorandum to ensure that I was starting off correctly. Specifically, I would address, in order, what exactly it was that they wanted me to address, no more and no less.

If there were a Statement of Facts required (usually in a Points and Authorities assignment), I would simply restate most of what the Memorandum already told me about the matter and then pepper in some more details, always thinking brevity. I figured that everyone knew the facts, since most of the story was on the Memorandum anyway, so the true point value here would be procedural, in following the instructions by creating the Statement of Facts, not substantive, in writing a treatise-style Statement of Facts.

Were the assignment just a memorandum or letter-style of writing, I would recreate the assignment Memorandum header and name of the attorney that had assigned me the task, or copy the name and address of the attorney that was going to get the letter, and open up with a lawyerlike introductory paragraph. I would always close it out with a lawyerlike paragraph as well. "Should you have any questions or concerns regarding this matter, please feel free …" You get the gist.

My issues would be always be underlined whether it was a memorandum, letter, or Points and Authorities-type assignment, and I would always start with the most relevant code, if any, followed by the most relevant rule or rules from the case or cases. Rather than write out the entire case citation, I would just put *"See Smith"* or *"Smith"* at the end of the rule. If there were two or three rules for the same issue and from different cases, and all were complimentary, I would just list one rule that best summed them all up and then put *"See Smith, Jones"* or *"Smith, Jones."* If the two or three rules were divergent, I would start with the one that favored my position first, analyze the facts, then list the other rule and analyze the facts in a contrarian nature, showing the reader why the contrarian rule did not apply in this instance. Since I didn't have this stuff written down on my outline in substantial fashion, as my outline was usually no more than one page in total, I would just pull the actual text of the codes or rules directly from the Library, as I had the page number written down on my outline and the required information highlighted or circled in the Library already, usually with a check mark beside it.

With issues and rules now down, I would make an analysis based on the facts from the File. Since again I had an abbreviated fact, name, or figure, or perhaps only a page number to refer to, I would quickly review these facts and or pull them verbatim from the File, then add them to my answer and apply them to the rule or rules.

This was pretty much it for me, unless, of course, there was something else that seemed like it should be in there (factors, judicial test, *dicta,* or holding). If it did, and if I had time, I would copy it from the Library into the computer directly. Remember, I usually highlighted this ancillary stuff with a different color to distinguish it from my codes and rules so that I could grab it and add it at will.

At the end of this, my conclusion was just that, a conclusion based upon the analysis of the facts as I saw them, or as I wanted the court to see them for the benefit of my client. When I did the MPTs and PTs, I endeavored to begin writing halfway through, or after 45 minutes of outlining or 90 minutes of outlining, respectively. I always wrote down the start time in the top, right-hand corner of what would be my outline just to be sure. Time flies when you're having fun.

This was a bare-knuckles system that I developed for myself and that ultimately worked for me and my particular flaws. Admittedly, this was really just a hodgepodge of differing methodologies and trial and, much error, but it was enough to allow me to write something that was seemingly competent and within the allotted time period. I knew that I was weak at the PT and was not counting on it to be one of my strong suits, but rather was counting on it to be just good enough so as not to prevent me from passing the CBX. If you are good at these, I implore you then to do a better job at them and make them fancier so that you can juice out all of the points available, particularly if you are not as good in another testing component.

By starting with the MPTs, I was not burning too many hours on this, and likewise, I was not killing my soul thinking about burning too many hours on this. I was also now reading and understanding and keeping my outline concise and free from a lot of manual scribe, favoring to copy the bulk of the information directly into my computer. I sometimes tried to outline directly into the computer, avoiding a manually written outline altogether. While this is superfast since you can cut and paste stuff wherever it should go, I was personally never able to get the big picture when assembling the pieces in this fashion. If you are able to write directly into the computer and put it all together in a comprehensive manner, then do you, but just make sure you end up seeing the forest through the trees.

After doing a bunch of MPTs and getting my bearings, I started to work the PTs again. Just like with the CBX essays, I was able to get my hands on several past PTs, both from Fleming's and directly from the Calbar website. Fleming's did a good job of compiling PTs in an ascending order from "easier" to "harder," and moreover, included a good cross section of differing PT types to ensure that the candidate had exposure to several possible scenarios.

While I never felt great about the PT, I also never gave up on it, got lazy, or left it up to chance. I did as many of them as I could, and modified and tweaked my approach until I felt as comfortable as I could. Ultimately, I realized that I would just need to be that much better in the other two areas (MBE and essays) to compensate. Remember, when I was inputting hypothetical scores into the CBX Score Analyzer, I would only go as high as 65 for one and as low as 40 for the other. This, since I knew that I was better at the memorandums and letter-type tests than the Points and Authorities variety, and I also knew that generally one of the two PTs on the CBX was more difficult than the other PT.

The first PT on day one was an objective memo, and I felt pretty good about it. I would conservatively give myself a 60. On day three, the second PT was a Points and Authorities that to this day I still don't understand. I ran out of things to write because I was so confused, but I kept writing anyway, trying to make it to at least a 50. Either way, I know that I didn't pass the CBX based on my PTs. Do the best you can with what you have and try to salvage as many points as possible to compliment your MBEs and essay scores.

Get your eyeballs on these as soon as possible and be sure and take a review course, preferably live and in person as opposed to home study. Don't listen to those who tell you that you can't study for this test since they are a "closed universe" examination, since what you can and need to do is practice the strategy which you learn in your review course. Do as many MPTs and or PTs as you can, or start with MPTs and work your way up to the PTs, if applicable, before the Bar Examination, and practice your technique. Whatever you do, don't allow them to interfere with the remainder of your studying, and if things aren't working out right, don't be afraid to make necessary modifications.

Remember, depending on your particular Bar Examination, the PT or MPT is likely the biggest headache with the lowest contributing point value. Nevertheless, always practice as many of these as you can and always under timed conditions! Just like the MBEs and the essays, candidates are notorious for running out of time, even with 3 hours at their disposal.

MEMORANDUM
To: Applicant
From: Timothy Miranda, Esq.
Re: Kiqaz v. Peetee

Multistaid

AS THE NAME would denote, Multistate Bar Examination questions are uniform in all jurisdictions that administer them. This uniformity means federal rules across the board and a majority of questions based upon common law, all with no state-specific questions. Likewise, all Bar Examination candidates take the MBE on the same day, the last Wednesday of either February or July. The test is comprised of 200 questions, 100 of which are administered in the morning, and 100 of which are administered in the afternoon. Each testing session lasts for 3 hours, or 180 minutes, meaning that the candidate has an average time allotment of 1.8 minutes per question. The Baby Bar tests 100 MBE questions in the afternoon, also with an average time allotment of 1.8 minutes per question; however, only the subjects of Contracts, Criminal Law, and Torts are tested.

Of the 200 questions that appear on the Bar Examination, 10 questions are so-called pretest questions, meaning that they are potential future MBE questions which are included in the exam merely to gauge their difficulty. Your raw score can therefore range from 0–190, since the 10 pretest questions are excluded from grading. There are no pretest questions on the Baby Bar, so all 100 are counted as part of the raw score.

Essay questions and the PTs are always a wildcard, regardless of your predictions or preparation. For example, if you look at the history of Constitutional Law essay questions on the CBX, they generally test on the more ubiquitous topics like Commerce Clause, Due Process, Equal Protection, and First Amendment. Therefore, if you write practice CBX essays in Constitutional Law, you will likely get fairly adept at writing about these particular topics. However, in what seems to be a new direction for the CBX in the twenty-first century, Constitutional Law essays have begun to contain questions related to much more esoteric topics, such as Executive Powers, Immunities, and Separation of Powers betwixt the three branches of government. Regardless of whether you had predicted a Constitutional Law essay, one of these topics may have been a curve ball. Fortunately with the MBE, if you do enough questions you won't strike out.

The MBE on the Bar Examination generally includes approximately 60 questions from previous examinations as a means of determining the difficulty versus previous administrations, or the so-called equating. I can remember taking my MBEs, both on the Baby Bar and CBX, and recognizing several questions that were mere variations of previous questions that I had practiced with in the past. I likely did not miss any of these questions, since I already knew the answers.

Of the remaining 140 questions, 10 are going to get jettisoned anyway since they are pretest questions only. You never know for certain which ones these are, but when you take the test, you have a pretty good idea. My MBE examination included some new-style questions that I had never seen before in any former, released MBE questions, such as grand jury questions in Evidence and mortgage questions in Property. The questions weren't that hard from what I remember, but they just seemed out-of-place based upon what I had been accustomed to practicing.

So now you have 130 questions that are not repeats of past questions, and likewise, they are not throw-away pretest questions. What are they then?

If you have been doing your practice MBEs, these questions will be just like every other one that you have been doing. Sure, names change, fact patterns are different, and the questions may even be asked from a different perspective. Fundamentally, however, the questions, and the law they are testing, are all the same.

When I started doing my MBEs in preparation for the Baby Bar, I sucked at them. Even still, I kept doing them, and then kept doing them again, realizing that the more I did, the better I would get. In this regard, MBEs are a lot like doing exercise, where the more you do, the more strength and endurance you develop. The more MBEs I did, the more readily I could decipher the question and determine what exactly it was that they were asking of me. As this skill developed, the more answers I got right.

When I took the Baby Bar, my congratulatory letter from the Bar Examiners included my scores on both the essays and MBE portion of the examination. On the MBEs, I got a raw score of 90 out of a possible 100:

Contracts: 27 (I told you I disliked Contracts)
Criminal Law: 31
Torts: 32

If I wasn't the highest-scoring candidate on the MBE component during that examination I was likely in the top two.

All considered, the Baby Bar MBEs for me were easy. Not easy at the time, but relatively easy when I began to study for the CBX and had to practice MBEs from all six subjects, Constitutional Law, Contracts, Criminal Law/Procedure, Evidence, Property, and Torts. Even still, the fact that I had done so well on the Baby Bar MBE questions gave me confidence that I could do well on the CBX MBE questions. More important, I had figured out the formula for success—do as many MBEs as you can, track your progress, repeat.

In preparation for the Baby Bar, I primarily used the Finz book and focused only on the three subject areas relevant to that examination. I also took a "test" of specific Finz questions as delineated by Fleming's, questions that were tricky or needed to be understood by the candidate. When I finished with this book I used a couple of other books which I bought independently and which were okay. When I finished with those books, I used the Fleming's book, focusing only on the three Baby Bar subjects, and also did the PMBR questions that were provided by Fleming's.

For the CBX, I used Finz's book and Fleming's book again. I also practiced on thousands of former MBE questions that had previously been released. These questions were also provided to me by Fleming's as part of my review materials.

The Finz book in many instances contains fact patterns and questions that are simply too long—much longer than those used modernly on the Baby Bar or Bar Examination MBE. As such, many of the questions actually seemed harder than those on the Baby Bar MBE, and ultimately harder than those on the CBX MBE. The PMBR questions were much harder than those on the Baby Bar and CBX MBE. This is actually a good thing.

The Fleming's book has a good cross section of questions on every subject, which is great if you get an MBE examination with questions on obscure topics, like the one I got during my CBX (mortgages). A lot of the questions seemed harder than the Baby Bar and CBX MBE questions. This is actually a good thing.

Naturally, the former, released MBE questions are a bit more concise and seem to be easier than any of the other commercially prepared practice questions, but my set was devoid of any answer explanation; just the correct answer denoted by a single letter. This is actually a good thing.

You see, the more you practice on the harder, long-winded, and even outmoded questions, the easier the actual MBE questions on your examination will become, as they will appear to be more concise and straightforward. Additionally, if you do enough of the outdated questions, you will even get good enough to spot any changed law.

In contrast, the more you practice with the former, released MBE questions, the better feeling you will get for the actual MBEs on your examination. If the correct answer in practice lacks any explanation as to why it is correct versus the other answers, you are going to have to figure this out by yourself. When you actually take the time to figure it out, you won't get it wrong again. If your Bar review does not provide these former, released MBE questions as part of your review materials, they should be available for purchase directly from NCBE.

While volume is the single biggest factor in improving your MBE score, just doing the questions en masse is not enough. In order to learn from your mistakes rather than repeating them, you must begin keeping track of every question that you miss.

In my case, if I did a set of 25 practice questions, I would make an "X" next to the incorrect answers on my answer sheet. I used a separate answer sheet so that I would not mark up my book, since I planned on doing these questions over again at some future time and didn't want to leave a trace of anything that would make it easier (or harder) on me during the next go-around. Instead, I just kept a separate list of all of the question numbers that I got wrong and from which source and subject they hailed, and retained these for a future redo. In addition, I would keep a running total, or tracking, of correct versus incorrect answers, and would keep tabs on these percentages.

When I started this process, I would always keep track of these numbers after doing an individual set of, say, 25 questions. However, I soon realized that these isolated percentages were deceiving. For example, if, for some reason, there were a series of several hard questions in a row, I might miss half (or more). On the other hand, if I were to do a set of 25 questions that were easier, I might not miss any. Since the MBE is itself a macroscore, not looking individually at what you scored in the morning session versus the afternoon session, or if in one particular block of 25 you missed half, you also must think big picture, and therefore, not get stressed out if the morning session seemed tough, or if you feel like you missed a few dubious questions in a row.

Using the example of a set of 25 practice questions, then, let's say that I missed 5 of these. On a percentage basis, this would be 20 percent incorrect. If I later did a set of 50 and missed 5, this would be 10 percent incorrect and so on. When I got to the end of any particular subject or section of questions, I would calculate my global percentage. For example, if a certain section had 200 questions total, and I did sets of 25 or 50 questions at a time, when I finished the entire 200 questions, I would add up all of the questions I got wrong. So, if, in total, I missed 30 questions out of 200, my total, or global percentage of incorrect answers, would be 15 percent. Assessing the percentages after you have done a couple hundred MBE questions is much more telling than assessing them after you have done a couple dozen.

Tracking your incorrect answers is therefore crucial, both for the purpose of reworking them again in the future, to ensure that you figure out what went wrong the first time, and moreover, for the purpose of knowing what you can expect to score on the Baby Bar or Bar Examination.

My own practice MBE scores prior to the Baby Bar were tracking at approximately 20 percent incorrect on those questions from Finz, and 25 percent on those questions from Fleming's. The PMBR questions were 30 percent. For the CBX, my practice MBE scores on the former, released MBE questions were tracking at approximately 12 percent and again 20 percent on Finz questions. The Fleming's book was at 30 percent, I imagine, since this time, I wasn't just focused on only three subjects. Again, these were global percentages based on a minimum of at least 200 questions.

The NCBE website has for purchase a couple of different online practice examinations which are comprised of 100 former, yet recent, MBE questions. When you purchase the examination, you receive a subscription that is good for 1 year, allowing you to go back and retake the examination as many times as you like. The examination can be timed or not, and you select the answer choice with your mouse as opposed to filling in a bubble with your pencil. Do this, as any opportunity to get your hands on actual, former MBE test questions should not be missed. Also, you want to get your mind and body accustomed to doing 100 MBEs in a single sitting, just like you will be called upon to do during the morning and afternoon of the last Wednesday of February or July.

I took the first one of these practice examinations about 2 months prior to the CBX. I missed 10 out of 100. I took the second practice examination about a week before the CBX. I missed 11 out of 100. My historic tracking of about 12 percent incorrect on the former, released MBE questions was spot-on, meaning that I was anticipating a raw score of approximately 165 out of 190 on the CBX.

To this point, the consensus among candidates seems to be that a raw score of 150 on the MBEs is really good, maybe because of the urban legend that if you score 150 or higher on the MBE, then they don't even grade your essays or PTs. Fortunately, I studied law from home and did Bar review from home, so I never got the memo and never set my sights so low. For me, missing 40 questions in total, or an average of 20 questions in the morning and 20 questions in the afternoon, did not seem like a good score. As a passer, I will never know what my actual MBE score was on the CBX, but then again, I knew what my score was going to be before I ever got there.

In addition to tracking and reworking and just plain doing a lot of MBEs, I always did the MBEs under timed conditions. While some people preach otherwise, particularly when the candidate is early on in the Bar review process, I always figured that a right answer is worthless if it comes at the expense of not finishing the examination on time. Although it may not sound like it, an average of 1.8 minutes per question is plenty of time if you practice under timed conditions and, well, condition yourself to the timing. Conditioning yourself means knowing internally when enough time is enough on any particular question, and making a check mark beside it in order to come back to it should you have extra time at the end of the examination. This is one of the benefits of practicing with the harder MBE questions that I mentioned above; they take longer than the questions on the actual examination, and therefore, your practicing on them will ultimately make you faster at test time.

On the Baby Bar, I remember finishing the MBE questions over an hour early. In fact, I had so much time left that I decided to go to the restroom (#1), then come back to my seat and recheck my answers. Before I get ahead of myself, let me share with you how I knew that I had so much time left and which answers I should recheck.

Since the MBEs are administered using a pencil and an answer sheet, there are no laptops permitted in the testing area for this segment, just as there are no cell phones, digital watches, or the like permitted in the testing area at any time during the examination. You can, of course, take in a small analog clock or watch, which is what I did for both the Baby Bar and the CBX. When I took the Baby Bar, the venue had a clock on the wall that I could see. However, when I took the CBX, there was no clock.

When the MBEs were administered on the Baby Bar, the first thing I did when the announcer said "Go" was to write down the time on the front cover of my testing booklet, the one that actually contains the questions. I knew that I had 180 minutes to complete 100 questions. I also knew that at 1.8 minutes per question, I should have at least 33 questions completed per hour (33 x 1.8 minutes = 59.4 minutes). Rather than look at the clock every few minutes and fret, I decided to do thirty-three questions and then look. When I did this I saw that I had gotten there in about 40 minutes, so I was well ahead of schedule. When I looked again around sixty questions, I was still well ahead of schedule and ultimately finished way early.

As I took the test, I made an "X" beside every question that I didn't feel 100 percent confident about. The idea was that I didn't want to spend too much time going over the same question multiple times and then running out of time later, since this may mean that one question could ultimately end up costing me five questions or more. Rather, I would come back and recheck that "X" question if time permitted. Time permitted, and some I changed and some I didn't.

On the CBX, I essentially did the same thing, except this time, I had to look at my watch every 33 questions or so rather than look at the wall (with no clock). In the morning session, I finished about 25 minutes early, and in the afternoon session, I finished about 35 minutes early. Both times I went back and rechecked the "X" questions that I had marked as suspect, and then exited the building posthaste.

I never would have finished early on the Baby Bar or CBX had I not always done my practice MBEs under timed conditions. Period.

On the CBX, with day one and day three dedicated to three essays in the morning and a 3-hour PT in the afternoon, the MBEs feel, or should feel, like a respite if you are adequately prepared. No need to write, no need to type, and you receive a forewarning of exactly what subjects will be tested and to what extent (quantity) that they will be tested. They even do you a favor of throwing out 10 questions which you probably missed anyway since they were different from anything that you had seen before. If this weren't enough, they put a cherry on top by including approximately 60 past questions from former examinations, all while providing you with thousands of former examination questions to practice with.

Do the MBEs the way that works best for you, not the way that anybody tells you that you should do them. For me, I quickly read the call of the question first, and then briefly scanned the four possible answers. I would then read the fact pattern, reread the call of the question, and then reread the answers. If I had to reread the facts or a part of the facts again, I would do it.

A raw score of 150 should be your minimum target score on a bad day. Set your sights high on this part of the exam and you will never be back.

How do I loathe thee, MBE? Let me track the ways ...

The Harangueover

WHEN YOU ARE studying for the Bar Examination 8-plus hours a day, 7 days a week (hopefully), there is not a lot of time for anything else. This is bad for your family, your job, your social life, and so on. Some pundits suggest taking a day off here and there, and others suggest taking at least 1 day off a week. I personally never took a day off, even though I got to the point where I was miserable and hated the thought of waking up early every morning in order to go through this whole ordeal again, and again. For me, however, this loathing was a good thing because it made me want to never, ever have to repeat this, which, in turn, got me out of bed early every morning.

Do what feels right to you, but be sure you achieve that never, ever feeling.

When the day of the examination, both the Baby Bar and CBX, arrived, I was confident, given all my hard work, and actually excited to be sitting, finally putting an end to the study madness that had essentially become my so-called life. The Baby Bar, although a 1-day examination, was over in a flash since there was no time to think about anything but the examination that day. The CBX, while 3 days in length, also seemed to fly by, given that I was either entirely focused on the examination, stuck in traffic trying to get out of the venue's parking lot, or crashing out from exhaustion.

For about a week after the Baby Bar, I had tried to postmortem the examination, rehashing the questions and my answers in my head and trying to figure out what, if anything, I had missed. Even though I tried not to listen, invariably, there were candidates that were talking about the issues (that they saw) when we exited the testing center, and some of these issues were not seen by me. This had me slightly concerned, not because I had a lack of confidence in my skills, but rather because as soon as the test is over, the fact patterns start to become hazy, and if you can't remember the questions with specificity, there is a propensity for self-doubt regarding the possibility of missed issues.

After the CBX, the first week was essentially the same as the Baby Bar, and unfortunately, there were again several candidates that were chattering about the issues as we walked out of the testing center (even in Spanish). I tried harder this time to avoid this, given that I had learned my lesson after the Baby Bar, yet, it is virtually impossible to do so when there are so many candidates jammed into one place. Self-doubt was greater this time since there were more essays, more MBE questions, and therefore, the fact patterns seemed to become hazy even more quickly.

While waiting for the results of the Baby Bar to arrive in the mail, I didn't get too preoccupied with the test after that first week had passed. This is probably because I was so behind with my 2L studies that I really had to get right back into the fray with no study honeymoon. Also, since the results would be arriving in the mail, the fact that they would just show up one day with the bills and junk mail made the anticipation more bearable.

By contrast, when the announcer at the CBX said, "Stop writing," and gave some final instructions to the candidates, he also happened to mention that the pass list would be available on the Calbar website at 6:00 p.m. on Friday, May 13. Great, Friday the 13th, as if the fact that you would know the exact date and time of your fate wasn't menacing enough already.

Unlike with the Baby Bar, 1 week turned in to 2 weeks and then a month and then 2 months. This time, I had no other studies to preoccupy myself with, and I had been studying so much that when it was over there was a huge void in my calendar. While this should have been great, I just couldn't stop thinking about logging in on Friday the 13th at 6:00 p.m., which meant that I couldn't stop thinking about the examination and what I may or may not have missed. I started inputting so many hypothetical scoring scenarios into the CBX Score Analyzer that I'm surprised it didn't blow up!

Even though studying, particularly for the CBX, seemed like it was one of the worst times of my life, the long wait and uncertainty postexamination was even worse. I share this with you because in retrospect, I wish I would have given some forethought as to what to do with all of my time once the examination was over.

Sure, I had things to do, things that I had not done while I was spending so much time studying, but by comparison to an 8–10-hour study day 7 days a week, this all seemed trivial. As for my company, I had delegated so much of my workload in order to create time for studying that, well, I realized how great effective delegation can be. No need to take the work back if it can be done better by someone else I always say.

When Friday the 13th at 5:59 p.m. came around, I went in to my home office and shut the door, wanting to be by myself when the results were displayed. I had thought so much about the examination in the past 3 months, and had read so many erroneous posts from other candidates on those law student websites, that I really didn't know what to think anymore.

When I found out that I had passed, I was actually disappointed in myself (after the initial exuberance wore off) for being so negative and succumbing to self-doubt. I shouldn't have been logging in to the Calbar website alone with the door shut, but rather popping bottles with models in an anticipatory victory party at the hottest club in town as my pass results were displayed live on a big screen while hundreds of balloons dropped from the ceiling. After all, I was a baller, a stone-cold Barrior, and not a buster.

Do yourself a favor and give some thought to life after the examination, because after all, there is still life after the examination.

Have that anticipatory victory party for me, candidate.

The Cradle Will Fall

THE FOLLOWING IS the 4-month study regimen that I followed in preparation for the Baby Bar. Please feel free to do more.

Month 1
- Purchased Fleming's home study review course for the Baby Bar, listened to all of the lectures, and created checklists for each subject.
- After the checklists were completed, I started doing all three of them daily, every day of the week.
- Concurrent with listening to the review lectures and starting to create my checklists, I began doing 25 MBEs (Contracts, Criminal Law, and Torts) per day, every day of the week.
- I wrote three essays per week.
- I would refer to my Baby Bar review outline and or my outline books from law school and modify my checklists as needed.

Month 2
- Daily checklists of all three subjects every day.
- 50 MBEs per day, every day.
- One essay per day, every day.
- Referred to the outlines as needed, modified checklists as needed.

Month 3
- Daily checklists of all three subjects every day.
- 75 MBEs per day, every day.
- Two essays per day, every day. I also started to write my essays without the assistance of an external keyboard since I was not going to use one during the examination.
- Referred to the outlines as needed, modified checklists as needed.

Month 4
- Daily checklists of all three subjects every day.
- 100 MBEs per day, every day. At this point, I began reworking the MBEs which I had previously gotten incorrect.
- Three essays per day, every day, no external keyboard. Also, I began to write the essays directly in the laptop examination software.
- Referred to the outlines as needed, modified checklists as needed.

Last Week before the Baby Bar
- Dedicated 1 day to a mock Baby Bar. At 8:00 a.m., I took four essays in 4 hours, but did not look at the model answers (until later). After an hour lunch, I did 100 MBEs in a scheduled 3-hour period, but finished early. The rest of the week I did the normal Month 4 schedule, redoing any essays that I had previously indicated as giving me problems.

I hit a home run on this exam because I spent so much time in the batting cage. Batter up.

See, Be, Esq.

THE FOLLOWING IS the 5-month study regimen that I followed in preparation for the CBX. Please feel free to do more.

Note: Since I had nearly 7 months to prepare until the next CBX administration in February, I did 10 MBE questions per day and one checklist per day, every day, until I was 5 months out. I still had these checklists from the Baby Bar and law school.

Month 1
- Purchased Fleming's home study review course for the CBX, listened to all of the lectures, and modified the checklists for each subject as necessary.
- After all of the checklists were completed, I started doing three of them daily, every day of the week, on a 5-day rotation.
- Concurrent with listening to the review lectures and modifying my checklists, I began doing 25 MBEs per day, every day of the week.
- I wrote one essay per day, every day.
- I would refer to my CBX review outline and or my outline books from law school and modify my checklists as needed.

Month 2
- Daily checklists of three subjects per day, every day of the week, on a 5-day rotation.
- 50 MBEs per day, every day.
- One essay per day, every day.
- Referred to the outlines as needed, modified checklists as needed.

Month 3
- Daily checklists of four subjects per day, every day of the week,

on a four day rotation. Given that there were fifteen subjects, one day would be comprised of only three checklists.
- 50 MBEs per day, every day.
- One essay per day, every day
- Referred to the outlines as needed, modified checklists as needed.

Month 4
- Daily checklists of four subjects per day, every day of the week, on a 4-day rotation.
- 75 MBEs per day, every day. I also took the first online MBE practice exam of 100 questions at some time during this month. At this point, I began reworking the MBEs which I had previously gotten incorrect.
- Two essays per day, every day. I also started to write my essays without the assistance of an external keyboard since I was not going to use one during the examination. I began to write the essays directly in the laptop examination software.
- At the beginning of the month, I started to review the PT materials, which, in hindsight, was too late (start earlier). I started to do one PT per week. After having problems with the PTs, I began to do two MPTs per week, usually on Saturday and Sunday.
- Referred to the outlines as needed, modified checklists as needed.

Month 5
- Daily checklists of five subjects per day, every day of the week, on a 3-day rotation.
- 75 MBEs per day, every day.
- Three essays per day, every day.
- One PT per week.
- Referred to the outlines as needed, modified checklists as needed.

Last Full Week before the CBX
- Monday: Dedicated one day to a mock essay and PT CBX. At 8:00 a.m., I took three essays in 3 hours, but did not look at the model answers (until later). After an hour lunch, I did one PT in 3 hours.
- Tuesday: I did my normal Month-Five study routine, but substituted an online MBE test of 100 questions for the normal 75 MBE questions.
- Wednesday–Saturday: I did my normal Month-Five study routine, plus one PT per day.

Last 2 Days before the CBX
- Sunday and Monday: Month-Five checklist routine and an outlining and review of every essay that had ever given me problems, going back to the very beginning of my review.

During the CBX
- At the end of day two, I reviewed the checklists of the essay subjects that I had predicted but that did not appear on day one of the CBX.

"I'm going to work so that it's a pure guts race at the end, and if it is, I am the only one who can win it."
—Steve Prefontaine, Track and Field Legend

www.ingramcontent.com/pod-product-compliance
Lightning Source LLC
Chambersburg PA
CBHW070556160426
43199CB00014B/2529